OUR BED IS FLOURISHING

Our Bed
is Flourishing

A Gynecologist Looks
at Sex, Love and Marriage

by ROBERT B. McCREADY, M.D.

SHEED AND WARD · NEW YORK

"Behold thou art fair, my beloved,
and comely. Our bed is flourishing."
—Canticle of Canticles 1:15

Contents

Introduction

This is a book about marriage. My justification for writing on this subject today in view of the massive amount of material on the subject is that I am giving voice to what my patients have taught me. I am not speaking alone and for myself. This book reflects my patients, the priests I have known who work with married couples, the couples in the Cana Conference of Chicago, as well as my own marriage. In addition, it is an expression of all I have read over the years on the subject. It is impossible to give credit to all who have contributed to it, because there are so many. The danger of neglecting some is too great to attempt any listing. In Cana work it has always been a tradition to borrow anything that seemed good, so I hope those who recognize their pet ideas will accept my thanks and gratitude. I owe my thanks especially to many of the clergy of the Archdiocese of Chicago. They are among the finest men I have ever known, and I could not have written this book without their help. My special thanks for suggesting this book and for encouraging me during its labor pains go to Andrew Greeley, William McCready and Nancy Gallagher.

When I had to decide who the audience for my book should be, the first group I thought about was the "about-to-be-marrieds." Then the hope of giving young married couples a glimpse of the beauty they might be missing prompted me to give advice to them, too.

I believe I have something new to say on the subject of married life. What I have new to say deals in depth with human life, because in marriage man and wife confront all life's problems in depth. Perhaps the title of this book should be *Our Beds Are NOT Flourishing*, because marriage counselors, priests and physicians know the tragic truth that marriages today are breaking up in too great numbers.

And the younger generation, despite its acute awareness of the human relations problems that parents poorly solve or evade, do not seem to be moving toward a correction of the situation. Indeed, because of their youth and their disorientation, they may compound the present tensions with newer ones. The couples who are to succeed in producing flourishing marriage beds must learn to be human in the fullest sense. Those of us who advise engaged couples or the young marrieds cannot approach the matter as sex experts or as problem-centered doctors. We must enter the situation as human beings, and we must use all the art and knowledge we can find. Above all, we must be aware that everything a couple does and is will be mirrored in their marital union.

Failures in marriage are failures of people. Perhaps this is why these failures are so devastating. Even the men and women who refuse to acknowledge such a failure as a tragedy, and who jump from one marriage to another in rapid succession are either putting up a brave front, or are going from one legalized liaison to another.

The one outstanding reason for writing this book is to attempt to bring some light on marriage, and perhaps to prevent a few problems from developing by helping young couples to become aware of potential difficulties. We hope that we can add a small impetus to marriage education so that parents who are unable to correct their own deficiencies will at least be able to avoid passing them on to their children.

We hope this book will help us understand what sex is and what it can do in both a personalized manner and as a means of reproduction. Perhaps we can come to understand reproduction as the responsibility which it is. Out of the morass of information and misinformation which comes from the mass media, we should be able to distill enough common sense and enough documented, scientific know-how to form a basis for a recognizable philosophy to apply to sexual relations and sexual matters. Excellent efforts are being made in scholarly studies of sex and sex practices; but, unfortunately, too many conclusions are made from inadequate samplings. The Kinsey reports are valuable studies of certain groups but cannot be used validly to speak of the American male or female.

This book is the result of twenty years in the practice of obstetrics and gynecology, plus a concurrent twenty years of deep involvement in premarital and marriage education. It is written with great fear and hesitation since so many works have been produced on woman—her nature, her sexuality, etc. What prompts this expression is the feeling that, despite all the effort expended, so much confusion remains. In fact, there is an axiom in medicine that, when many different cures are proposed, the chances are that none of them will prove particularly beneficial. I would like to present women as I have seen them, to pass on what they have told me and what I have learned from them. Since I am an active obstetrician interested in marriage problems, and since I do a certain amount of public speaking on the subject, I meet problems and expressions of problems that might not be available to other investigators. A discussion of marriage problems based on this broad experience should have some usefulness and validity. Since I am a Catholic and have lived through the years of high birth rate and rhythm counseling, I have a unique entrée to the material on this subject, too.

The accounts of couples with marriage problems is not meant to be a comprehensive view of the marital state, because emphasis is on those in trouble. Their stories are presented as case histories, and my purpose in writing this book is to present some experience and thinking, not to present solutions. If I can provoke thought and reflection rather than provide solutions, I will consider this book a success. If such reflections result in disagreement, this is still worthwhile. If I give real help to someone headed for disaster, this book will be well worth the work I have put into it.

OUR BED IS FLOURISHING

1 Marriage at the crossroads

Human progress—there is no other—depends on individual efforts, which are at the same time its tool and its result.

—Lecomte du Noüy

Supportive institutions of the past

In an older, tradition-bound society the sexual role was clearly prescribed and well understood by most people. Certain things were expected of a man; and the woman, in turn, had a well-defined role to play. He was the breadwinner, the provider and the disciplinarian, while she raised the children and ran the household. Together, they were responsible for teaching the children the rules of society and training them for the roles they were to play. This was true only for the middle and upper classes, of course, and for those of the lower strata who sought to emulate this pattern and move into the group. It applied primarily to the Western Judeo-Christian culture. Even among this segment there were infinite variations, but the pattern was essentially the same.

The male might engage in affairs, but they were usually with "bad" women, primarily professionals. He was always

3

secretive about his affairs and never discussed them in public. The double standard applied, and punishment for his transgressions was not as swift and as complete as it would have been if his wife had sinned. Transgressions by the younger generation occurred, and, as usual, young people followed in the footsteps of the adults. Human behavior in 1912 was probably not much different from today; the number of illegitimate children and of abortions was about what they are now, when correction is made for growth of population; but the rules were clear, and punishment was fairly consistent for those who were caught.

One outstanding exception to this behavior pattern was the amount of conversation and writing on the subject of sex. A generation ago the whole matter was swept under the rug. There were very few studies on sexual behavior. Extremely serious problems, such as venereal disease, were just breaking into print in medical circles; and we should note that in that era medical knowledge and controversy were not covered in newspaper columns the way they are today. It was not until 1936 or so that newspapers began to print articles on venereal disease. The process of sweeping things under the rug was more complex than the simile would indicate. This "rug sweeping" was a form of group repression in that there was an attempt to bury it mentally. In a sense, the mass mind was engaged in the mechanism of repression and was suffering from the frustration of hidden mass guilt.

To put it in a simplified form, people were lying to themselves, and they were having the usual difficulties, because lies require a massive amount of effort. Truth can be left alone, but lies have to be tended and watched, or else they break out. A lie has a reproductive life and grows with age. The longer it is suppressed, the bigger it gets, and the more likely it is to breed other lies. Finally, the burden of maintaining it becomes unendurable.

A young man might have had visions of some "nice" young lady as a sexual partner, but according to the standards of that time, he cast such revolting thoughts out of his mind. This was the repression that Freud was writing about. The individual was ridden with guilt and frustrated by repeated attempts to maintain his balance. Slips of the tongue, unconscious actions and recurrent dreams embarrassed him, forcing him to use stronger methods of holding these thoughts down. He lived in constant anxiety lest his hidden thoughts come forth and expose him for what he thought he was—an evil person.

Defects of the system

Gradually it was discovered that many defects existed in the system. Venereal disease was prevalent and reached into all layers of society. I remember a young boy of fourteen who was operated on during my internship in the 1930's for acute appendicitis. He came from one of the better families in a most exclusive section of the city. By accident a blood test for syphilis, which was required only for patients sixteen years old or older, was reported positive. Investigation revealed that he had been seduced by his mother's maid. It was only too apparent that he had received no sex education whatsoever.

It is interesting to note that in this era, which is looked back upon by so many as a time of pastoral peace and tranquility, it was necessary to put drops of silver nitrate in the eyes of newborn babies as a routine procedure in order to prevent blindness caused by gonorrhea transmitted from the mother. Doctors also regularly performed blood tests for syphilis on all pregnant women, all adults admitted to hospitals, and on those getting married to detect cases of syphilis. The largest number of syphilis cases are transmitted by promiscuous sexual relations.

Apparently the rules were being broken ruthlessly by large numbers of the so-called respectable elements of society, and many innocent and ignorant victims were infected by people who did not know what the tragic consequences of their actions would be.

Since the 1930's, society has moved fast and very far. Many of the older generation do not like some of the things that are happening today; but we should never forget that the impetus for all this change came from mankind's desire to improve, not only his own condition, but, especially, his children's welfare. We started on this road because we believe that in a free society the only way to regulate behavior is to provide all the facts which will help people make informed, intelligent decisions. Some of our present difficulty may be blamed on our lack of decision. We have not gone far enough in providing education, particularly in the sexual field. Now we are confronted by the old dilemma of too little knowledge too late to be of value. We reiterate the claim that sex education is best conducted by the parents in the home. On paper, this is excellent theory. In practice, and in the quiet security of my office, sixty percent of my patients admit to having inadequate knowledge for their own sex lives; and they do not feel at all competent to provide it for their children. Time and again, workers in the fields of sociology and psychology are showing that such education is not being given in the home. Perhaps it is about time we admit that most parents do not feel capable of giving their children sex education, or they are reluctant to carry out their obligation for other reasons.

This might be a good time to point out that we must be

careful to keep in mind certain facts about human nature. One of the paramount items which must concern us is our ability to gloss over the truth or to tell an outright lie. If you are dealing with a parent-school organization whose members accept their responsibility for sex education and this attitude is considered to be the "in" thing, you cannot expect these people to admit their inadequacies in public. If you ask for a public vote on a subject, even by secret ballot, many who feel inadequate will react by compensation and aggressively defend a policy they could not possibly follow. A survey of such a group will produce similar results. If you were to hold private interviews with each couple, you might not reach true answers, because the mechanics of setting up the interviews would bring about defensive reaction.

Many teachers and some physicians know how these parents feel, because they have been asked to instruct a child by a worried parent who, in his or her concern for the child, forgets pride and admits inadequacies. Surveys of sex knowledge possessed by children have shown glaring ignorance of some of the simplest concepts. This indicates that the parents have done little or nothing to fulfill their role and responsibility. The reason that so many parents neglect this phase of their child's development is not laziness or lack of concern. It is simply a twist in their personality which prevents them from handling this quietly and peaceably as it should be done.

Communications media and the sexual revolution

Our modern era has opened the floodgates of information and allowed free discussion, but many have found ways to use this freedom for their personal advantage. The greatest offenders are, of course, the advertisers. They have found that sex sells.

So the pages of our newspapers and magazines are open to discussion of sex. Ads portray the human body and show contact between boy and girl, man and woman; sexual stimulation is promoted in the most subtle and clever ways possible, but with no view toward the long-term consequences of such stimulation on the vulnerable young. Clever psychologists develop techniques to get attention and transmit a message. The items overtly advertised may be cars, perfume, books, clothing, but the media use sex, girls, love, play, to sell the cars, perfume, etc.

This blatant use of sex in advertising carries over into the entertainment world, into newspaper stories, and assaults the ears and eyes of all who live in today's world. Add a little sex and it sells. The results are rather obvious and best expressed by an Englishman in London during World War II. "The trouble with the Americans is that they are over-rich, over-sexed, and over here."

This overemphasis produces some obvious and drastic effects and interferes with the educational process. We might better say that it becomes a part of the educational process over which we have no control. The whole movement of liberal sex education was developed to protect the individual and society, to produce responsible adults better prepared for marriage, and able to avoid the severe emotional trauma which results from careless sexual affairs. The sexual information so beautifully and subtly presented to anyone capable of looking at pictures carries a simple, destructive, and tragically wrong message. It keeps saying sex is for the young and beautiful; sex is a lark, something for a date, a relaxation, a trip to nowhere and back.

Never in all this fantasyland will you see a homely girl; yet I believe it was Harry Golden who said that some of the world's most beautiful loving was done by homely women. I have rarely seen a "glamour girl" who developed adequate sexual response in marriage, and I have often read in medical literature about the syndrome of glamour girl frigidity. Sounds like heresy, doesn't it? How tragic and yet how simple. Emphasize attraction in women—as though men needed such stimulation—but never touch on the subject of a woman's capacity to respond to sexual activity, which is really the key to her role in this duet.

The destructive element in the advertising or entertainment approach to sex is that it contains a philosophy. The copywriters and scriptwriters would ridicule this, claiming they know little and care less about philosophy. But that is the point. Knowing little and caring less, they infuse it into the social body with no caution or reservation, and with little or no long-range sense of responsibility. Sex is for the young—do it now—sex is fun and games. This is rarely said, but it is always implied. It is never out in the open, but it underlies all the pictures and all the copy.

Never in this fantasyland do they portray the sexual love of a skilled twenty-year marriage, nor the deep love of the fifty-year marriage, compounded of sexual love, pain and suffering, and their total life experience, of which sexuality is such an integral part. None of these voices will tell of the pattern of growth which exists in a good marital-sexual situation, as the functioning of intercourse changes in the marriage over the years. None speak of the factor of development in the female, of her growth as a woman, and of her changing response to intercourse, which is so dependent on the husband. Nothing is said about the learning process between husband and wife, or about the creativity required, or of the sacrifices which are so inherent in the process. No one can expect a Picasso or a Bach to spring forth from nothing; but the idea of a "sexy" woman still prevails, and man continues to imagine that he will find fully grown what only he can give birth to.

So now we have our poor modern only partially educated, highly overstimulated, and with certain ingrained tenets, which will handicap him tremendously in his future growth. He may have some thoughts on how to live for and enjoy today, but he doesn't know how to structure his life for to-morrow. He may know a few things about sex but nothing about sexuality. And he certainly hasn't any conception of sexual growth and development as a long-term support for marriage and a family.

Inadequate education

In addition, we grant him freedom, or to be more exact, we push him into the arena before he can clearly see. We place boys and girls in the same school system, a system not actually designed for either of them. We launch them into a social system, which is not organized or equipped to do anything or provide anything for them, so why should we be surprised when they create a world of their own?

As one example, we know that girls mature emotionally earlier than boys do. Yet our system provides no way for a boy of twenty-four to meet a girl of nineteen except in a bar or in certain church social groups, which attract a very small segment of the population. Dating is centered around school events, and the combination of severe necessity (must have a date for the Fall Dance) plus limited availability of partners produces the peculiarly unnatural phenomenon of going steady. I say this because I believe most young people do not really enjoy going steady. They put up with it because of the se-curity it offers them.

A mother of six grown children who was at one time the belle of our college days provided another interesting sidelight on going steady. She contended that an impetus was given to the whole practice of going steady by the techniques used by orchestras at dances. When we were younger, a band played for about three minutes and then paused, allowing a change in partners. Today, bands play fifteen or twenty minutes and then take a break for five or ten minutes. In our time we would take any girl to a dance, because there was a good deal of changing of partners and no one got "stuck" too long. Twenty minutes is a long, long time on a dance floor; so it is wise to know your partner well and not risk someone new.

Going steady, freedom from parental supervision, plus the mobility provided by the automobile, adds up to a very dangerous situation. Add to this an increasing use of alcohol among young people, and the situation becomes explosive. If we face the problem honestly, we should have admiration for the high quality and good sense of the majority of our young people, because they avoid serious trouble as well as they do. I believe we should congratulate both young people and their parents for the excellent efforts they make in a basically bad environment.

It is true that the post-World War II generation of parents has tried harder to help their children than almost any generation in the past. We have been labelled a child-centered society, and to a great extent this has been true. More books have been written, more meetings held and more suburbs built with the children in mind than seems possible; but much of the effort has not produced the results desired. It seems apparent that we are preparing our children for the world we came from rather than the one they are going to live in, and that some of our improvements are more destructive than beneficial.

Another disruptive factor is the increase in awareness among the young. Our many dishonesties have been exposed, so we have been labelled "phonies." Our insistence on premarital chastity despite our own failures in chastity and our extolling of marital virtues that we violate repeatedly results in a generation chasm rather than a mere generation gap, because young people are both idealistic and intolerant.

To sum up, our modern young people live in a free, open environment where little support is given to a sensible pattern for growing up. Too many decisions are required of them at too early an age. A massive amount of information is poured upon them with a technical finesse that is fantastically capable. Tremendous educational tools are called entertainment and allowed to range in a completely free manner and with the utmost irresponsibility. If some poor teacher tries to initiate a calm, intelligent discussion on premarital intercourse, the town or neighborhood will rise up in wrath; but a movie can show the subject in the most lurid, stupid and incompetent manner, and little or nothing can be done. National television can run a program in which a professional criminal abortionist is allowed to portray himself as a savior of humanity. So parents must either keep TV sets under lock and key or attempt to discuss this complex subject with a teen-ager.

I am not making a plea for censorship. I realize that for adults such open discussion may be the lifeblood of modern democracy; but I am trying to point out the paradox of trying to educate the young in fundamentals at an early age, and at the same time expose them to complex questions, which really belong at the end of the course.

Public argument is a good thing, but a disagreement among

teachers in front of the pupils destroys the educative process. This is no demand for censorship of the communications media. I am not even asking for more responsibility on their part. However, I am pleading with media directors to try to imagine the confusion of our young people and to realize the conflicts they are experiencing. We all must increase our efforts in both schools and homes to counter the babble of voices in the market place, and to help our young people sort out from the mass of opinions the basic principles they want to live by.

Pressures imposed on human relations

Marriage is such a vital part of human effort that we must look closely at all of the factors which can affect it. Years ago when couples had a shorter life expectancy, marriage until "death do us part" did not last as long as it does today. Many couples married ten years or so and afflicted by tensions that threatened to sever their union may have stayed out of the divorce court, because they thought that, since life was short, they might as well stay together and make the best of it.

Today, forty-year-olds have a future to plan—a future as long as thirty to forty more years—and so they must learn to adjust to the problems they will have to face when they are in their seventies or eighties. Young couples will live much longer than their parents did, and during their lifetime they will face many more complex situations than their parents or grandparents faced. They will live in small apartments in crowded cities and will shop in large centers at a distance from their homes. So they will lose contact with the friendly neighbors and corner grocery store their mothers knew.

Shrinking space and cramped intimacy impose greater pres-

sures on human relations. The turbulence of change adds to
this pressure, and the expanding crisis reaches further into the
depths of the individual's psyche. This disordering of the relations of person and environment is straining our society's
ability to care for the casualties which appear in our mental
clinics, our divorce courts, our juvenile courts and our criminal
courts. Most of this disruption centers on the family and on
its internal functioning, since this is still the prime educator
for our young.

Another factor in promoting and accelerating the crisis in
family life is the increase and spread of education. In our age
more information reaches more people at a greater rate of
speed than ever before in history. This increase in the depth
and width of education has more repercussions than almost
anything else that has happened. We teach our young people
more about the other people who live on this planet and about
those who lived in the past, so they become acquainted with
other ways of living and begin to question their own way of
life. The protection once provided by isolation and insularity
is lost. In the past, rules could be imposed simply by edict,
without argument or discussion. Today, we want our young
people to raise questions and develop true understanding; so
we teach them to question even the most firmly established
principles. We cannot expect them to stop at a certain point.
When students have learned about other cultures that fostered
sexual promiscuity and lived without monogamous marriage
and its painful restrictions, what is more natural than for them
to question the right of society to restrict their natural desires?
When they ask for a complete explanation and a re-evaluation
of all sexual standards, why are we surprised?

The hippie movement in the United States is an example of
this demand for freedom from social and moral restrictions.

A medical history of the hippie movement in San Francisco, for example, would include coughs, colds, an epidemic of serum hepatitis from unsanitary common use of needles in drug taking and an epidemic of venereal disease.

High school youngsters talking about the "flower children" in San Francisco will have to know about gonorrhea and syphilis in detail. Edicts and moral precepts alone are ignored and must be backed up by facts. If childhood ignorance is thereby destroyed, we will just have to accept the loss and realize that the price of ignorance in this complex world of today is a terrible one.

The younger generation wants truth and honesty, and the older generation wants to preserve some guidelines to prevent disaster. The younger generation can point to countless examples of hypocrisy, sham, materialism, destruction of human substance itself, both psychic and soma, by a system built on compromise, prudence, acceptance of falsehood to avoid trouble and innumerable other sins.

The older generation can point to increasing signs of disaster arising out of the new freedom applied without knowledge, restraint or foresight. Perhaps each generation has to learn the hard way by making its own mistakes. But many of us believe that man advances by standing on the shoulders of the giants who went before him, and many of us feel that man is a reasoning being who can anticipate problems and solve them.

My answer is to give the younger generation the honest answers they seek—all the answers. They are capable, and their education is immeasurably better than ours; so we must throw off our old habit of avoiding discussion of certain taboo topics. They want truth, and they must have it. So talk of sex must include the heartbreak as well as the joy. The older generation's restraint, which led many highly successful and sexual parents to keep their joy a delicate, private thing, may have to be lifted so that their children can learn how this joy could have been shattered by an extramarital affair or stopped in its infancy by premarital intercourse.

Our schools must participate in the sex education of young people by planning marriage courses, which will include discussion of the problems presented in various television programs, films, songs, etc. Much of this could be done by individual teachers as a part of courses in literature, history, sociology, etc. Other efforts would be best presented in a more formal structure.

Whatever the method we use to teach young people the joys of unselfish married love, most of us agree that we must teach them that all social systems must have some limits. We don't have to revert to Puritanism, but without limits we can drift into hedonism and debauchery as did many cultures of the past. History is full of sects of various sizes which destroyed themselves by giving vent to primitive and sadistic drives. It is not enough to break things down. Destruction does not satisfy; revolution dies in its own violence. We must continue our search for new values and for ways to present and increase understanding of old values. All our hope lies in the younger generation. If we cannot make them understand the meaning of true love, we will be forced to become spectators of a holocaust repeated so many times in our history, and our future will be a loveless void.

2 The engagement, honeymoon and early years of marriage

Some power in a man compels him to run away from and to get rid of himself. It drives him to wanting to escape from his own presence. . . . Loving means achieving something, being filled with a spirit which is related to the one which inspires artists and priests. It is creation, like the work of the poet or prophet.
—*Theodor Reik*, Of Love and Lust

Most girls start dreaming about weddings when they are about four years old. They continue to plan and dream until their wedding day. So they should be warned that any discussion of sex with men can be dangerous, since the talk can change to action so easily. The fact that she is willing to discuss the subject can be interpreted to mean that she must be "that kind" of girl. The intellectual approach is the favorite gambit with some "wolves." It is a fairly obvious approach to anyone who has a minimal amount of experience.

What is not so apparent is the girl who finds she is constantly running into the wrong kind of men, because every date makes a pass at her. Of course, her appearance or actions may invite this kind of disrespect. The male tends to type his women into good girls and bad girls, one touchable and the other untouchable. The modern male may be able to quote Freud, Ellis or Kinsey; but, despite that veneer of sophistication, he is still a human being. So he is subject to temptation. Although he may speak of love, he is thinking of sex.

Love and sex

Too often, love and sex are equated, because they are so often found together. This should never happen. Love is definitely a product of culture and can in no sense be called an instinct or an appetite. In love, the individual emerges as a distinct person; in purely sexual involvement, the individual is not important.

When he is in love, a man does not see his beloved as a particular individual of an attractive gender; he sees her as a unique person. Our difficulty in discussing the word "love" is that it is over-used. The particular misuse that concerns us at this point is to describe the infatuation of a pair of sixteen-year-olds by the same word used to describe a beautiful fifty-year-old marriage, or even an excellent ten-year-old marriage.

There is no disagreement with the statement that love and sex are often found together. They certainly do exist together, often in a symbiotic relationship where the one strengthens the other. Some of the greatest love stories are tinged with sexuality, and I doubt that any sexual relationship can be mutually satisfactory for very long without the support of love. The point is that, despite the intimate association, and despite the fact that they are often found together, love and sex may coincide, but are not identical. Coincidence is not evidence of identity.

When I was a young student, my home town had streetcars. On every car there was a motorman and a conductor. One rode the front, and one rode the back of the car. Since I lived at the end of the line, I often rode the car alone, helped with changing the trolley and even drank coffee in the small lunchroom at the end of the line. I can never remember seeing them apart. Conductor-motorman was a unit to me. Yet I was never confused about the fact that a motorman drove, and a conductor collected fares.

Love and sex are similar. Love drives; sex collects the money. Sex is instinct, a biological need bound to the body; while love is of the spirit, not localized, not identified chemically, but still a definite emotional relationship. There is a tremendous difference in the treatment afforded the object of these two functions. Sex may be casual; love never is.

After satisfaction, the object of sex may become boring or even hateful. This could never be true with love. In a crude and too often masculine sense, the sexual partner can appear as an appendage of one partner's sexual parts—as an object. In love, the object is always seen as an individual or a person. Sex is selfish and uses the object in order to obtain satisfaction; it wants a woman. Love is discriminating; it wants a particular woman and will accept no substitute. Love can exist without sexual desire, and it can outlast sexual desire.

If any points are vital in establishing and promoting an enduring marriage relationship, they are that romantic love is a destructive force, and continuing creativity is essential for good and durable unions. Romantic love is a wonderful, a thrilling, a soul-shaking experience; but when romantic love is the total approach to marriage, it becomes devastating.

Far too many young people feel that falling in love, or being in love, is all that one needs. After the legalization or consummation of the union, they feel nature must take its course.

20

Herein lies the error, because nature's course is not what they think it is or desire it to be. When a person says he is falling in love, he is really getting to know someone. This compound of knowing and of burgeoning sexual attraction is the lovely elixir the poets have sung about for so many ages.

This does not demean love in any way. What is obvious is that the feeling is fragile and exhaustible. In particular, knowledge of the partner must wear off and slow down. It is true that throughout life one continues to find new aspects and new insights about one's partner, but the discoveries come farther and farther apart and become less impressive as life goes on. For too many people marriage degenerates from this point on. It becomes merely a working partnership without spark, and boredom increases year by year. Such a union does not grow in strength as the years pass, and it is much more easily disrupted and torn by conflicts.

If we take an honest view, we accept the springtime fancy with the awe and wonder that we feel when picking up a newborn baby; but we do not block out of our minds the adult who lives in this infant. We know that spring must be followed by summer, and the joy and success of summer depends, to a great extent, on our own creativity and hard work. When we love, we act. When we love, we assume a commitment to do something. How and what we do depends on our humanity, our capability for loving, our humor or any other human quality.

Sexual relations between husband and wife can partake of all these qualities, and because of them the couple can grow each year. They become stronger, more expressive, more sustaining to each other and more sexual. The successful married couple looks back on the experiences of the early years as wonderful, pleasant and rather childish. Their success stems from their unique and individual growth in sexuality. This growth is biologically oriented in the sense that a woman's ability to respond in and to the sexual act is a product of time and other multiple factors. It is not an entirely spontaneous entity, as is the male's potency and capacity for orgasm.

Sexuality is a mysterious and fascinating relationship, which changes progressively through the years; it expands and matures to a point undreamed of by the cheap portrayers of flashing lights and bursting rockets. Those who use it for various purposes outside marriage on a multiple encounter basis could never imagine or portray its expansive capacities, its increasing intensity, or its all-pervasive influence on a relationship between male and female.

This is the "sex act" versus "sexuality" theme, or what has been referred to as "push-button sex"—an attempt to bind behavior to form, to focus on technique rather than emotion. In this view of marriage, sex can become the epitome of rights and duties, the cure for every problem and the yardstick by which one measures love. It is true that there are couples whose sexual relationships leave much to be desired, and yet they achieve a high level of compatibility, joy and happiness. Sexuality is a product of the relationship, not a cure-all or an end-all. Orgasm is a by-product of a good union, a good relationship between two people whose psyches have been allowed to grow without too much hindrance.

To focus on the achieving of pleasure or the occurrence of orgasm is self-defeating. When a person seeks pleasure for itself, it becomes elusive. Pleasure usually results only from activity that can be appreciated as it occurs. When one strives for perfection in actions as complex as this one is, the striving often interferes with the very things which can do the most to bring out the results desired.

This is why the centering of interest on techniques can become so frustrating, and why success comes so often to those who worry less and enjoy themselves more. Sex without a loving relationship that extends over days, months and years may succeed as mutual masturbation, but not as sexual intercourse. A useful loving relationship is the way to a mutually satisfactory sexual pattern unique for this couple—one which strengthens their marriage, while it enhances their sexuality in an expanding fashion.

A difficulty inherent in writing about marriage is the ease with which the writing becomes too serious and fails to convey the humor and joy which should be present in any good relationship. A loving union must incorporate all of humanness, and humor and laughter are most uniquely human. In writing, it is so easy to become imbued with the suffering or problem marriages and to fall into a pattern of prevention, of trying to avoid the pain. The reader must never forget the need for laughter and fun. In truth, the aim of this book is really to attempt to demonstrate that being married is fun, and that it can continue in this vein throughout life. The joy a couple take in each other and the lightness in their relationship combine to maintain a spark that puts a glow in their eyes and a spring in their step.

Each man and woman carries his or her past within themselves. Their memories go back to childhood, to the time when the differences between male and female were first recognized. Their memories are so persistent that often they live in their memories instead of in real life. They re-enact their childhood memories in an automatic, non-deliberate manner. The man may have such vivid memories of his mother who used a chronic sickness as a means of controlling her family that he plays her role instead of his own. Dr. Cornelius Lan-

sing presented such a case in his article, "Medical Aspects of
Human Sexuality."

The wife, on the other hand,

. . . portrays to herself the long-suffering, neglected girl, while
assigning to her husband the role of her coarse, lazy, incompetent
father. Each is unaware that the other is writing a different play,
and neither has access to the real list of characters in which both
are cast as overgrown children trying to be adults, who can't
escape from their past family relationships and are now busily
and tragically recreating them in the present. Saddest of all, each
partner resists any tendencies toward maturity in the other, and
tries to coerce him into truly living the assigned neurotic role.
Whenever the husband grows up a little, the wife uses her knowledge of his sensitivities to cut him down to size. If the wife becomes less disagreeable, the husband does all he can to push her
back into her neurotic role.*

Many other cases taken from my own practice illustrate how
the past can move up into the present and wreak havoc with
a relationship between a man and his wife. Steps can be taken
to avoid such a situation. When the young man first becomes
aware of a girl as a person who may become important in
his life, he should begin to develop a pattern of sexuality designed, not for a moment, but for a lifetime.

Premarital intercourse

Since this is a relationship of mutuality, her actions are also
important. We are not dealing here with equals but with two
unique individuals of different sexes who have dissimilar reproductive systems and sexual response patterns. He may have

* Dr. Cornelius Lansing, "Medical Aspects of Human Sexuality," *Clinical
Communications*, Vol. I, No. 4 (December, 1967), p. 34.

a strong urge towards intercourse or other forms of sexual gratification. She is more interested in being needed, in being loved and in striving toward a permanent union. Fear of desertion or loss is paramount in her category of worries. If she complies with his request for sexual activity of either a partial or complete nature, she is more likely to do so to please him than for her own pleasure, and this may be antagonistic to any real sexual growth on her part.

Premarital sexual relations are no problem to the male; he fits into this pattern with ease. He is comfortable in a sexual relation without responsibility and would just as soon keep it separated from reproduction. It furnishes him with what he needs—relief from frustration, reassurance of potency, and, at least temporarily, a weapon against loneliness. It builds up his image of himself and helps, for awhile, to make him feel more like a man. It gives him the feeling of accomplishment, of victory over life and the feeling that he has climbed the mountain and can now rest on the peak.

What about her? Why did she go into this relationship in the first place? Will it combat her loneliness? Will it make her feel more of a woman? Perhaps it may for a very short time; but once the glow of knowing wears off, where can she derive any satisfaction from a temporary relationship, which denies the essence of femininity, reproduction? The pleasure in the act itself will not mean anything to her after a while, because whatever orgasm she might be able to achieve will not be adequate; and it will deteriorate quickly as the relationship becomes static or starts to go downhill. Without severe sexual frustration to obtain relief from, she is denied this value.

Most women who cling to these unions do so either by pretending it is a marriage, or by fastening hope on the thought that he will eventually grow to need her and will marry her.

She will become overpossessive to overcome loneliness, and this overpossessiveness, combined with petty jealousy, may drive him off. The lack of children, or the impossibility of having any, is a sword driven into the heart of her creative femininity. Every pill she takes, every time she inserts a diaphragm or sees him use a condom is a twist in the wound.

If he controls his urge and allows the interpersonal relationship to grow, maintaining physical contact on an affectionate level, her faith in the duration and depth of the relationship will expand; and she can answer him with more natural sexual responses of her own. Her horizons will widen, and her security will begin to develop. Now the male must make some crucial decisions. As her faith in him and their relationship increases, her sexual feelings will grow in strength and intensity until the male may have to be the controlling factor. He should control her emotional expression, because of his love and concern for her as a person. He knows and appreciates her prejudice against premarital intercourse and the danger inherent in such activity. He realizes that to take advantage of her would produce feelings of degradation and guilt and cause pain and suffering. These disadvantages would far outweigh the immediate pleasure he would enjoy.

The inhibitions we desire to impose here are truly elastic, soft and gentle. They are the restrictions love imposes. Love sets aside selfish desires, because of concern for another. As the relationship progresses, the man learns that heavy petting, or even coitus itself, is of less interest to the girl than to him. This makes the man more restrained. He has learned by watching the changes which have occurred in her sexual response during the past few months that she is undergoing development, and that she will flourish and become a genuine and sexually responsive woman if he is only willing to wait. He is beginning to realize that this is a unique opportunity for him to learn to help her grow. We must remember that she is not a piece of clay or plastic to be molded but a person to be loved and understood. Those hours of talk that lovers engage in should enable him to get to know her as the child she once was and still is, to know her parents as she saw them and some of her ways and feelings. As he becomes more aware of her and what she has been, he becomes more conscious of the inhibitions, fears and fantasies he must learn to live and cope with.

She, in turn, must participate in this relationship by keeping communication as open as possible. She must understand his need for physical expression of his love and try to understand it as a form of language which ultimately can say, "I love you" in a much deeper sense than even the world's greatest poetry. She must learn to trust him and depend on the durability of the relationship as he shows himself sincere and understanding.

The engagement

As the relationship continues into the engagement period, which I would define as beginning when both partners are in agreement that a marriage is going to take place at a more or less definite time, more emphasis will fall on physical compatibility. It is in this period that a great deal of premarital intercourse takes place.

To many behaviorial scientists this is really not sexual promiscuity, and in a certain sense it is really not premarital intercourse. The explanation lies in the fact that the essence of a marriage is the contract between two people. The contract is fulfilled when the marriage is consummated by sexual intercourse. In the strictest interpretation of Canon Law in the Catholic Church, a non-consummated marriage can be annulled and declared no marriage. This can be done only if very conclusive proof can be offered that intercourse did not take place. Conversely, what I am implying is that two people who have agreed to marry complete the act of marriage, or seal their contract, by premature consummation. This act is not legally binding under Canon Law; but I think it is in the meaning of the law, if not the letter. Although their act may not be as dangerous or as detrimental as some other activities, there are many marked disadvantages in having premarital relations. One of the most important is that it renders the wedding ceremony meaningless. It reduces it to a farce in the eyes of the bride, particularly if she also happens to be pregnant.

Another disadvantage is that the surroundings and physical conditions of clandestine affairs are rarely, if ever, a proper setting for beginning a lifetime of loving. The woman is dependent on mood and atmosphere, so that waiting for the honeymoon is well worth the pangs of unrequited desire.

If the act of intercourse was really her idea, and if she were sexually developed enough to enjoy it thoroughly, perhaps this wouldn't be true. However, most premarriage consummations are accidents. The man either lost control or was not concerned enough about the woman to restrain himself. The woman is more vulnerable in this period, because she feels less fear of desertion since he has committed himself to marry her.

Another large group of engaged couples fail, because they are far more human than they realize. Because they have a great deal of experience in physical intimacy, stopping just short of coitus, they overrate their own power of self-control. In various premarriage courses I have advised young couples to impose stricter limits upon themselves as the wedding date approaches. I also stress the importance of consulting a doctor at least three of four months before the wedding date for a physical examination and to ask any specific questions they may have concerning the honeymoon and first intercourse. Doctors who specialize in obstetrics and gynecology, or younger general practitioners, are usually well prepared to give advice.

The honeymoon

Our couple has survived courtship, quarrels and the wedding ceremony. Now what about the honeymoon? Honeymoons are necessary. They need not be extensive or expensive, but each couple should go off by themselves. This should not be a vacation with places to go and things to do. It should be a state of mind with privacy so they can grow together. Admittedly, there is embarrassment, tension and fear for both. Maybe that is why so many go to resorts with planned activities all day and dancing all night. By burying themselves in activity they avoid facing each other. Upon returning home, they can retreat to job and other recognized separations and live peacefully, they hope.

Honeymoons are for getting to know each other and can be a borrowed apartment, or even a borrowed room. We have already implied that sex itself often fails on the honeymoon. Pain and no reaction for the bride, premature ejaculation or failure of erection for the groom are common occurrences best treated by ordering another bottle of champagne. If the groom finds that after ten days or two weeks he is unable to penetrate the vagina, he should consult a gynecologist or interested generalist. Because the opening of the bladder in the female is between the vagina and the symphysis pubis, some brides have a problem of frequent urination and slight burning on urination called "honeymoon cystitis." This will often subside spontaneously with an increase of fluid intake. Only occasionally will it be persistent enough to require medication.

The man's role on the honeymoon is one of the most wonderful examples I know of to illustrate what it means to be a man. He must be firm and yet patient, responsible and mature, yet playfully persistent and adaptable, full of fire and still under control, all at the same time. He must be thinking and planning every moment and yet be romantic and free; he must keep his mind on what he is doing and remain conscious of the long-term effects of what he does. He must be forceful and gentle, demanding and yet capable of allowing the whole affair to subside until a later time. All of the ingenuity and tenderness he can muster will be repaid a thousandfold for the remaining years of his life.

Technically a few points can be of help. If the wife is not able to use a lubricant, he can use a small amount of a water-soluble jelly on the glans penis to increase the ease of penetration. As he attempts actual entrance or intromission, he should make sure that the labia minora, or lips, are separated in order to avoid inverting them and causing pain. These are folds of skin lying on each side of the vaginal entrance and running from back to front. They can be separated rather easily by using the index and middle finger to spread them apart, while the penis is brought toward the vagina and against the hymenal ring. It is assumed that the ordinary male-above position is being used, with the wife lying on her back and his face down above her, supporting his weight mainly with his elbows and knees.

Once he feels the ring of the hymen offering resistance, he maintains pressure with the forward thrust of his hips in a steady even manner, occasionally increasing it as long as discomfort is not too marked. He attempts not to lose ground at any time. In other words, if the lady protests, he may avoid an increase in pressure; but he should not give up any gains he has made, if at all possible. By maintaining pressure against the ring, a gradual increase in the diameter can be felt until a point is reached where the husband can be certain a final effort will succeed and can act accordingly. Once penetration is accomplished, no movement should be made, for a time, if pain is present.

The early years of marriage

The early years of marriage union are crucial in the way that all beginnings are important. It is not so much that mistakes are made. These can be forgiven and left in the past. But a tone is set, and a style is developed; and these are more permanent and more influential. Fortunately, love and biology combine to produce emotional support and motivation to keep these two people as one; and, with help, this union will grow in strength as years go by.

Assuming that the will to succeed exists in this marriage, and that there are no serious psychological impediments, the main help our couple needs is communication between them. Books such as this are a help in that comments and knowledge can be placed before them for selection. But every couple has its own unique problems, and very few solutions work for all. The young wife needs to learn that her husband's sexual drive is different from hers; his urges are more intense, and his motives are not necessarily similar to hers. She quickly finds that his ego is brittle. What she considers a polite suggestion, he calls nagging and responds to with anger. When she wants some particular sexual technique changed, she may find it easier to assume the role of a sexually ignorant, incompetent female. In the course of the conversation, she may mention casually that there must be something wrong with her, because she does not respond to his rapid, aggressive masculinity.

About two weeks later he will come up with a subtle, indirect and slower approach, and he will spend hours afterwards telling her how this wonderful idea hit him. I do not believe that I am being a traitor when I admit that man is basically stupid about sex. His biology is such that he is almost bound to be too blunt and too fast. Fortunately, he is curious, and he manages to learn.

She could be more cooperative and not maintain that long, stony-faced hurt silence for days when he asks what he did wrong. Perhaps she does not know and doesn't want to get analytical about it. We can thank our creator that man was made curious. Once he senses trouble, he is stubborn enough to vary his technique and watch for improvement.

In the course of these early years the male animal has to grow antennae. He must develop sensitivity to the nuances of female emotions, which are somewhat foreign to his ordinary living style. A good example is the word "no!" or various actions which mean the same thing. He proposes intercourse by word, deed, look, by a flat request or by some delicate ploy. She acknowledges his signal and indicates understanding. So far things are going well. Sometimes she plays dumb, and he knows that she knows what he means; but this time progress is definitely being made. Physical contact is made, and she responds to his lovemaking. Then when he is certain that there is no doubt, she says "no" in no uncertain terms. There are pleas, excuses, frustrations, perhaps even a serious quarrel; then a wonderful process of making up. Reviewing the affair later over a cigarette in bed, she completely dumbfounds him by indicating that he was pretty dumb not to recognize that her "no" didn't really mean "no."

I have never seen any intelligent explanation of this phenomenon, and I am not sure I want one. Once you learn the rules and develop the fortitude to take a few rebuffs, this becomes an intriguing and even enjoyable game with some of the most precious rewards life can ever give. This is a part of love—accepting people for what they are and enjoying them for what they are. Women are flighty sometimes, exasperating occasionally, but lovely and never boring. Just about the time you think you have them all figured out, they do something else so puzzling that you have to start all over again.

She feels the same way about you. Despite all the propaganda, the female is not the romantic one. She is the most practical, cold-blooded, routine-ridden creature in the world; and once a sexual relationship has reached a certain point, she wants to relax and keep it that way. The door is locked; the light in the bedroom is out. She is wearing that silly nighty she thinks is so pretty. He goes along nicely to the point where she is really getting interested, and that wonderful, glazed look is coming into her eyes, when he stops, turns on the light and wants a cigarette. The conversational interlude is fun, but now he wants her to get rid of that nice nightgown and wear those silly black pants he bought. No need to go any further. Sometimes it fails, but often it works; and later she lies in his arms full of drowsy contentment and gratitude and wonders where he gets all these crazy ideas. "Aren't men silly boys, but aren't they just absolutely wonderful!" she asks herself.

This is marriage. This is the union that produces a couple. This is what they need when their child dies, when he loses his job, when any other big troubles strike them. This is what the lineman and the pot rassler were lonely for.

A COUPLE*

He was in Cincinnati, she in Burlington.
He was in a gang of Postal Telegraph linemen.
She was a pot rassler in a boarding house.
   "The crying is lonely," she wrote him.
   "The same here," he answered.
The winter went by, and he came back, and they married.
And he went away again where rainstorms knocked down
     telegraph poles,
And wires dropped with frozen sleet.
And again she wrote him, "the crying is lonely".
And again he answered, "the same here".
Their five children are in the public schools.
He votes the Republican ticket, and is a taxpayer.
They are known among those who know them
As honest American citizens living honest lives.
Many things that bother other people never bother them.
They have their five children, and they are a couple,
A pair of birds that call to each other and satisfy.

As sure as he goes away she writes him, "the crying is lonely".
And he flashes back the old answer, "the same here."
It is a long time since he was a gang lineman at Cincinnati,
And she was a pot rassler in a Burlington boarding house.
Yet they never get tired of each other. They are a couple.

* From *Good Morning, America*, copyright, 1928, 1956, by Carl Sandburg.
Reprinted by permission of Harcourt, Brace & World, Inc.

3 Feminine response to intercourse

This bud of love, by summer's ripening breath
May prove a beauteous flower when next we meet.
—Romeo and Juliet

At this point we reach the heart of the matter, the cause of most problems and the remedy. It isn't that women are so important as much as it is that man has been so blind and so very foolish. Many of the earlier views on sexuality were developed and maintained entirely by men, and a great deal of this outlook continues to pervade modern liberal thinking. This is what I call male-centered sexuality. This is sex as the male animal wants it to be, a toy or plaything. They see women as subjects to be enjoyed as they enjoy good wine, food or music, and the more beautiful the women are the better. They call her "sexy," because she is attractive and because she stimulates men. They place all the emphasis on a woman's ability to arouse what often seems to be a lagging male, and to drive him into a frenzy; but nothing is ever said about her capacity to respond. Yet the nature of her sexuality is her response to intercourse.

Certainly all those other qualities are attractive, but without

34

sexual response from the female, the whole frenetic activity becomes a cruel joke, a parody on masturbation, a self-centered type of sexuality in which the male floats from woman to woman. This search for the right woman is usually doomed to failure, because in most women sexuality develops with time, care and love—above all love. It isn't a question of finding the right person at all. It is a question of planting a seedling in the right soil, tending it, watering it and helping it grow. Support and encouragement will make it bloom into a creation unique for these two persons—a precious possession that represents years of loving tenderness and effort.

In attempting to write about this particular subject, we face the immeasurable and boundless variability of the human person. Women come from many nations, cultures and backgrounds and each reacts differently to similar situations. I am limiting my discussion to the modern American woman and her sexuality as seen through the eyes of her doctor. Sexual activity is related more to the appetitive functions than to the instinctual and has two main reasons for existence: procreation and pleasure. It is with the second of these two that we are concerned at present, although the first cannot be completely ignored and intrudes extensively into the woman's feelings.

Sexual pleasure for the woman consists of the capacity for responding to stimulation by sexual arousal and the ability to continue through this process to sexual orgasm. The female body has certain areas which are more sensitive sexually than others. These are usually the mouth, breasts, lower abdomen, inner surfaces of the thighs, the genital areas, and, in particular, the clitoris.

Stimulation of these areas, usually in a progressive manner, moving from the least sensitive toward the more responsive, produces lubrication of the vagina and its opening, along with tumescence or swelling in the labia and para-vaginal areas. In a condition without inhibitions such as marriage, the increase in excitement level will cause the woman to demand further stimulation, concentrating more on the mons (the area just above the hard bone at the lower part of the abdomen). This brings her into what has been called the plateau phase. This is a particularly good term since she often desires to remain at a certain level before attempting to go higher or farther.

In contrast to the male, whose aim may be to get there without delay, she may want to fool around a little bit. It is in this area that the man requires a good deal of sense and sensitivity in order to find his way. A good part of this foreplay will involve clitoral stimulation, and it would help if the male realized that the tip of the clitoris is very sensitive and excessive stimulation can be uncomfortable, just as excessive stimulation of the glans penis can cause discomfort. The shaft of the clitoris is less irritable, and activity should be concentrated here. Following a proper amount of preparation, the penis is inserted in the vagina and the stage of intromission begins.

Vaginal and penile stimulation are both accomplished by an in and out thrusting motion which rapidly produces orgasm and ejaculation in the male, and, unfortunately, only gradually produces orgasm in the female.

The speed and the depth of the thrusting motion is usually of an increasing rate and amount, a crescendo effect. This is effective in producing the male orgasm and may, in fact, be a necessity. In other words, many men can continue for a longer time if the rate is slow and the depth of the thrust is limited. This control and variation can be extremely helpful in overcoming the slower response rate of the female.

The female orgasm itself is, when it occurs, similar to the male as far as sensation is concerned. There is a build up of nervous tension and energy to a peak with a dramatic sudden release of this energy and a subsiding relaxation into a normal resting state. We are speaking here, of course, about the fully developed female reaction, which might be seen only after some years of marriage and after having passed through various lesser stages of development.

Feminine orgasm

Feminine orgasm is confusing because, although it resembles the male reaction in many ways, particularly anatomically and physiologically, it differs in many other important and more subtle respects.

Before we enter into this portion of our discussion, I think it is time to tell my readers that all of my knowledge has been obtained from some very wonderful women—my patients—who have managed to put up with me for so many years.

I am discussing the typically virgin female starting a licit or socially approved sexual relationship. The early reaction to intercourse is not an orgasm. There may be a great deal of excitement, pleasure, thrill and wonder, but I have never had one patient married two years or more who thought the wedding night was anything but plain misery, or a wonderfully humorous and childish attempt, to be looked back upon as a delicious private joke.

In the early months of marriage, provided the situation is right, she gradually develops more ability to respond to love play and reaches greater heights of arousal. Finally, on some wonderful occasion, the roof falls in and the bells ring. Actually, the feminine orgasm is almost pure sensation and probably the most consistent description given by a patient is, "I know I have finished."

Modern sex manuals sometimes confuse more than they assist, because of a too vivid and overly dramatic description, which leads the woman to see that her reaction is nothing like the book; and, therefore, she must be frigid. Reactions vary tremendously from patient to patient and from year to year. The only thing that is really important is whether or not she has "finished."

Any attempt to describe orgasm is fruitless; it is like trying to describe all of the paintings in the Louvre. One mature, sexually developed married woman will have a variety of reactions during a year, ranging all the way from a quiet slipping down a children's slide to a crash over Niagara Falls. The most characteristic description is her definite assurance that it has happened. Admittedly, she becomes confused by reading and by trying to compare herself to others; but when she sticks to her own feelings and assesses the difference between the present and the past, she recognizes a point where a change occurred, and "it" happened. She also recognizes a point where a change occurs in the character of the orgasm, as we shall see later. She is insistent in her description of it as something new, a different type of reaction "much better than before." This is the biological-psychological component of the development we have discussed, the growth or the maturing of sexuality.

A second major difference in the nature of feminine orgasm is its increase in frequency and intensity with the passage of time. I have used the term "sexual development" to describe this. A woman's sexual reaction is a matter of development from little or nothing to sometimes extreme heights.

If one were to make a chart or graph of the variation in sexual response in the marriage relationship over a period of thirty years, the male's line would be almost level. In other words, the intensity of his own orgasm is of a fairly constant nature. His is what could be called an all-or-nothing reaction. A woman's chart would start at a zero level and gradually move higher over the years until her intensity of reaction could become stronger than his.

When this stage is reached, we can say that the marriage has matured sexually. Naturally, her reactions continue to vary, and at time she reaches no orgasm. During her period of growth the early reactions may be quite infrequent, but as the level of intensity increases so does the frequency of the occurrence. This is probably because she becomes more capable of response, and also because her husband becomes more adroit in sensing her moods. Because she responds, he becomes more secure, more assured and more capable of selecting the proper time, etc. He becomes more capable of being continent, of abandoning a more or less hopeless endeavor in order to await a more propitious occasion.

A third line might be placed on the chart indicating a woman who does not achieve orgasm. Her line would start at zero and perhaps rise slightly, but then it would fall off to nothing or to a very low level, well below that of her husband. This would indicate little or no growth in response.

This has been called frigidity, but I wish to enter a vigorous objection. When the bride's husband is stupid, inconsiderate and incompetent, why should she be called frigid? If her father was a neurotic, sex-obsessed puritan who planted fear of sex in her from the day she was born, why should she be called frigid? The experts have recognized this for some time and have covered their embarrassment by saying, "There is no such thing as constitutional frigidity." This means that no women have been born frigid. In other words, there really is no such thing as physical frigidity—there are just undeveloped females. I would define frigidity as an aversion to sexual intercourse, a more or less persistent antagonism that defies the best efforts of the husband and the wife; and it is usually psychological. Some cases of frigidity require intensive psychotherapy. Despite my objection to the word, I will use it for lack of a suitable substitute; but I hope my meaning is clear. Sexual inadequacy, or lack of response on the part of the woman, is a matter of development. The longest I have seen a patient wait was eighteen years. This woman was obviously distraught and very reluctantly admitted that she had orgasm for the first time in her marriage. The reason for her very severe apprehension was that she was rather well-read and felt certain she was developing nymphomania. This is an almost psychotic desire for intercourse that is never satisfied, and it makes the victim compulsively and blatantly promiscuous. It is very rare. I spent about one-half hour listening to her story and explaining to her that she was a normal human female, even though somewhat delayed in her development. She comes in regularly for cancer smear tests and has never brought up the subject again; and I have never questioned her about it. Judging from her appearance and demeanor, however, she is a happy woman.

Many married women fall into a class whose sexual development has been slow and whose reaction to intercourse inadequate. Some may have tried to change this, and perhaps have questioned a doctor, who may not have been interested in the problem, or was embarrassed by it or even incompetent to discuss it. Then these immature women lost the desire to change things, and now they have begun to tolerate intercourse as a burden. Many of this group never consult a doctor. They are detected in practice only when they are told that coitus may be resumed at a certain time following childbirth or pelvic surgery. They answer casually that it really makes no difference to them; they would just as soon stop completely if they could get away with it.

Clitoral and vaginal orgasm

Another difference between the male and the female reaction is that the latter, in its early stages, is often multiple. The woman places emphasis on the clitoris as the center of orgasm. The multiplicity of orgasm means that, if the foreplay is continued long enough and the clitoris is properly stimulated, the orgasm will hit several peaks. The same thing can be accomplished with prolonged intermissions or continued afterplay. As the process of development continues, some patients will notice a marked change in the character of orgasm. The center of interest becomes the vagina and the reactions are seldom, if ever, multiple. Case histories of my 900 patients—all married at least two years or more—show that seventy-two patients had noted a distinct progression from clitoral-centered reaction to vaginal-centered reaction. Actually, it doesn't seem to make that much difference to the patient herself, because her main concern is about her husband and how it affects him. The well-loved woman partially derives her adequacy from pleasing her husband. She certainly is far more disturbed over sterility than over failure to respond to coitus. One might say that orgasm is orgasm, and satisfaction is satisfaction; and one can help people, not by arguing how things should be, but by showing them how things are, and by helping them understand themselves and each other. The whole point of bringing up the argument of vaginal versus clitoral reactions is merely to add biological-psychological validity to the growth concept. I want to show that marital sexuality improves, or can improve, with time and love, and to re-emphasize that sexual responsiveness for the woman is part of the total relationship, not a point of technique. When a woman is loved, desired and treated with true consideration, she isn't overly concerned with the particular orgasm. None of the latter are truly consistent, as is the male's orgasm; and despite years of success, some complete failures occur. A husband secure in his masculinity will apologize for failing to help her "go all the way." She will shrug it off with, "Don't worry, we will have other nights." This is love.

The vaginal reaction is important in that it represents an advanced form of female sexual response. Since it is more dependent on psychological and spiritual values, it fosters a greater relatedness of persons. The wife feels gratitude toward the husband who brought this gift. This feeling of relatedness centers on the two in one flesh, the penis in the vagina, and it reduces the general sex play with tongue or finger to just what it is, a playful beginning, a pleasant background, which leads to this moment of moments when these two rise to heights that are far beyond words, when their bed is really flourishing.

In a more completely developed or vaginally centered orgasm, clitoral stimulation becomes more quickly uncomfortable; and the woman may demand that the period of foreplay be somewhat reduced and the length of intromission increased. Most patients have stated that in the beginning of vaginal orgasm development, ten or fifteen minutes of intromission was required to bring about orgasm. Later this may be reduced to five minutes or so. Obviously, the time factors are estimated.

There are not that many science-minded couples around, thank God! Much of the argument about the existence or non-existence of vaginal orgasm has become needlessly acrimonious. One group insists on having objective evidence for a difference, and another group leans on the more frequent prevalence of the clitoral reaction. All evidence for the existence of vaginal orgasm comes from patients who are in a free interview environment. They are usually quite expressive in indicating a specific point of transition from one reaction to another, and they freely admit that, once a vaginal reaction does occur, it will not remain consistent. They do not seem upset when it fails to appear. The older clitoral reaction is still considered highly satisfactory. Either is good, but the vaginal is considered more rewarding. They do not seem to know just what produces this reaction except that they often mentioned that "things were going very well." The feeling seems to be that success is related to the general well-being of the marriage rather than to any particular technical points. Some highly-responsive women are capable of achieving a clitoral reaction during foreplay, and then a vaginal reaction during intromission. They are most specific about the difference. The fact that vaginal reactions are not too common should not surprise anyone. Experts in any field are usually uncommon, and the number of truly great marriages will not be any more frequent than the number of truly and fully human people.

I realize that the concept of vaginal orgasm has been derided in recent years, and that modern research such as that done by Masters and Johnson indicate no physiological differences apparent in the type of orgasm. My statements are based on those women in my practice who have indicated that the development of their reactive capacity was a progressive one and that, at a very specific time, a transition occurred. When this happened, they describe the reaction as being more centered in the vagina, never multiple, and more complete. They were insistent on indicating a marked improvement, and on the fact that it changed their attitude toward their husband and toward sex in general. It made them become more involved sexually and more of a partner in the act. The important thing is the progression in the female's development, the increase in the durability of the marriage union, and the improvement in the depth of communication. Now they speak the same language.

Many years ago, a thirty-two-year-old patient, who had been married seven years, consulted me regarding some minor gynecological problem. I saw her on a very busy day, and since her case was somewhat routine, my notes on the chart were very sketchy. In the course of the examination I found that she had a partial paralysis of the muscles around the vagina (childhood polio), and I showed her some exercises to strengthen them. About two months later she made another visit. As she walked into the room, she looked at me with a glint in her eye and said, "What in heaven's name did you do to me the last time?" Since the notes on the chart were so sparse, I really didn't know, and I began to have all sorts of ideas of malpractice suits and court appearances. Stalling for time, I carried the conversation and, finally, the story came out. Her sexual development had been very good, and as she practiced the exercises, the vagina became more sensitive and more capable of muscular response so that a vaginal reaction resulted. The point is that she recognized a very marked change and was extremely vivid in her description, despite the fact that she was a rather shy and modest woman.

Another differential point about female orgasm of either type is that both are all-pervasive. The man centers his feeling in the penis and perineum, while the woman describes the

reaction as going through her whole body. I remember reading
at one time a fictional statement by a woman character, "I
feel all around you." This is echoed in many ways by patients.
"It feels all through me." "I explode all over."

Of the many dissimilarities between male and female sexual
physiology, the relatively slow letdown of her reaction is the
cause of more silent resentment on the part of the wife than
any other. Whether a woman has had an orgasm or not, her
feelings and her physiology subside slowly. If she has been
sexually aroused but failed to reach orgasm, this letdown can
be very prolonged. When orgasm has occurred, no matter
how intense, she goes through a rather long afterglow. She
may want to retain the penis in the vagina for some time, and
she will usually want to be held and fondled quietly. Practically no woman would complain of orgasm failure if her husband would recognize this need to allow the emotions to subside in an atmosphere of love and sustenance, instead of going
to sleep while she stews in resentment. It is rather ironic that
a man would do this, because he can readily put himself in a
similar situation; and he certainly knows how he would feel,
and how he would like to be treated.

I have had little experience with the following complaint,
but many couples report it frequently, and it causes apprehension. They complain that it is a struggle to achieve simultaneous orgasm. My advice would be to forget it. It is one of
those rare accidents that is worth breaking champagne over.
That both can achieve orgasm is enough; to be simultaneous
is rare indeed.

Another fallacy is the belief that once a woman learns to
react, she should react consistently. I suppose this is part of
the male-centered sexuality—anything we do she has to do.
Female orgasm is inconsistent and fragile. The cry of a baby,

a turning door knob or any noise will make her forget husband, sex and everything else.

Some years ago during a time of early marriages and an acute housing shortage, many young brides lived with in-laws or parents. Their introduction to marriage was absolutely atrocious. One wonders what made their parents forget their early years of marriage. As one young bride said of her folks, "The least they could do would be to go out to a show once in a while."

Couples living under such conditions, and those with growing children, must expect such disruptive events and should do everything they can to control the situation. Locking the door provides some security; utilizing a time of the day other than the evening, and various other means are all in order. One means that should never be forgotten is the recurrent honeymoon, mother and father off alone. Each couple must solve its own problem and fit it into their own economic level. Even a weekend in a nearby motel can be days of wonder and joy. Sometimes I get the impression that many couples feel such activities are immoral. If more couples used these facilities, perhaps there would be fewer jokes about couples in motels.

Another sector where the fragility of woman's reaction is obvious is in the question of mood. The male's sexual drive is lessened, or even abolished, by overwork or nervous tension, but the woman's capacity is potentially spoiled by countless little things.

Man has trouble understanding this fragility, because his actions are more muscular. They actually reach a point of no return, when he is oblivious to anything else. The house could fall on him, and he would not be aware of it.

One final comment on this particular aspect of sexuality:

the male, after intercourse and orgasm, has a feeling of relaxation and accomplishment. He has done something; he has won the race. The woman, after orgasm, has a feeling of gratitude, particularly to the husband who brought this gift of gifts. She is relaxed and has the desire to sleep, along with a feeling of a special, intimate attachment to the husband who has done this for her. Is it any wonder that many feel this is such a great part of the cement that makes the marriage last? When one is aware of the tremendous volume of sedatives and tranquilizers that are sold in our country each year, it makes one wonder what is going on. An observer might conclude that our marriage rate is very low; that very few people are having intercourse; and that we are all the result of more or less spontaneous combustion.

The last thing I want is to have someone consider this a how-to-do-it book. No one can teach others how to achieve happiness or even how to obtain simple satisfaction. What we do is to provide vicarious experience. Herein lie some of the problems others have met and a few of the ways in which they have lived through them. Directions, tendencies and certain modes of reacting can be illustrated, but the individuals have to choose their own special twists and turns in finding the right path. Many of the guidelines have been laid down in earlier chapters. Now specific attention will be focused on certain things.

In our technical society we want our directions to be clear and concise, and we expect results; but this is an art that must incorporate all of a person's humaneness, or it will be worthless. If we stumble in trying to explain it, please accept our apologies, for the task is difficult. Our point of view will be mainly that of the man approaching the woman, although this will be reversed when it seems necessary.

Sexual technique and approach

Certain areas of the body are referred to as erogenous zones.
For both sexes, the genital or pubic areas are highly sensitive.
The mammary or breast area of the female is also erogenous.
The tip of the penis, particularly the undersurface, is probably
the most sensitive area for the male; and the clitoris and the
area just above it, the mons pubis, are the most sensitive areas
for the female. The clitoris is a small, erectile (capable of
becoming somewhat rigid) organ lying just under the symphysis pubis (the hard bone at the lower pole of the abdomen).
A lengthy description has been offered regarding these areas
of the body, but there is a world of difference between technical discussion and application. This is emphasized very force-
fully in counseling more intelligent and academically oriented
couples.

I have been completely baffled by well-meaning and well-
read young people who know everything they should, but
who seem to be too serious and seem to be struggling too hard.
This is not a contest. This is living. One doesn't enjoy a beautiful day in the country by trying; one just does. It is good
to know where to go and how to go, and it is wise to pick
the right day and the right company. But once the chemistry
is mixed, the rest just comes. So, too, with lovemaking. Being
in love, knowing what has been pointed out here, and learning
with each other, should be a joy and not a struggle.

Becoming enmeshed in technical details is one of the most
self-destructive approaches there is to sexuality. If two "experts" are to engage in a form of mutual masturbation, this
might work. They could become skilled in sex practices and
might even give each other a few kicks, but this is not sexuality.

This form of expertise has no life of its own, and it dies when the novelty wears off. This is not the joy inherent in sexuality, and such technical ability is wasted on a real woman who wants to be a person, not an object.

In describing the female erogenous zones, a progression was mentioned from the less stimulating to the more stimulating zones. It started with kissing and moved on to clitoral stimulation. This cannot be done mechanically, and I suppose it really cannot be described. How do you kiss a girl? We are talking about love play, and both words are, or should be, full of poetry and dreams. The human female body is one of God's greatest glories, and some of mankind's greatest artists have failed to paint an adequate picture, let alone tell us what to do with it. Patience, love, time, a sense of humor and imagination are the teachers; and there is no hurry, because we have years to learn. The mutuality mentioned before plays a large role here, because this is lovemaking for two people; and conversation is a great part of that which we are seeking. No approach should be silent or automatic. Time out for a short lull and a heart-to-heart talk is a part of the beauty, and it adds to the pleasure and success of the biological union.

As noted previously, there is a difficulty inherent in trying to describe lovemaking. Even as simple an act as kissing is a task for description by the best of poets. The man in love has the entire universe of the female body to explore, and such a task is a part of his lovemaking. Provided he has the proper attitude toward her and is sensitive enough to recognize the effect he has on her, there is no limit to his activity. When he is imbued with love and concern for her, his attempts to transmit this feeling to her by way of his fingertips and hands is assured of success. Holding her hand, stroking her cheeks, ears or neck while kissing her and telling her what she means to him can be an excellent beginning. As the conversation proceeds his hands can speak to her breasts, now soft, now firm, now near the nipple, and now along her flank and back. Just as she seems to like one area, he moves to another in a tender mood of teasing. The rigidity which appears in the nipple is an indication of her response. As this conversation becomes more involved, the language is shifted to her thighs, particularly the inner surfaces, and finally to the vulva, the clitoris, and the vagina itself. The pace and variation must be based on the response or directions he receives, and, like any conversation, cannot be stereotyped. What happens must happen, and love is our director. With some apologies for being trite, a woman should be handled as the lovely creation of God which she is.

It must be obvious that control on the part of the male is a large factor in the success of sexual technique, and the need for this cannot be overemphasized. The ability to achieve a pace suitable to the response cycle of his wife, to pause and help establish a mood, to control the sexual and biological urge in order to maintain the spirit of love demands control. Throughout the whole relationship the male is constantly fighting his basic drive toward copulation, his concupiscence. His failures will be frequent, and time after time his wife's needs will be forgotten as his masculinity asserts itself and completely overrides all other considerations. As long as he supports her through the withdrawal, the detumescence stage, or the letdown, she will not condemn him, because she recognizes the effort he has made. In a perverse way she glories in his masculinity and in her power to produce this rather room-shattering reaction. When this release of masculinity can be contained and freed to coincide more or less with her peak, the heights have been scaled. Life will never again be the same for these two people.

As years go by there is less need for the male to slow down his response, because the woman eventually begins to react more quickly, and because the communication or signals between them become more efficient.

Later in marriage, control is used to avoid starting anything at the wrong time and to aid in the practice of continence which will be required sometimes in all marriages due to illness, mood, pregnancy or visiting relatives. As the union grows, the man begins to realize that coitus when she is not interested is not worth it, and it destroys what they have been building. He definitely does not want her to learn to *tolerate* intercourse, or to put up with what was once called woman's burden. He may reach a point where, in spite of a fair start, he finds things are just not right. Although he may have reached a high peak of stimulation, he stops and tells her, "You're just not interested."

She may be shocked, because she has steeled herself to accept him despite her lack of response, and she will react in either of the following ways:

She may feel relief because she does not have to tolerate something she can usually accept with joy. She also feels gratitude for the consideration he shows her and the sacrifice he is willing to make. Such gratitude is an important part of the cumulative effect which finally results in married love of the deepest and most inexplicable nature.

A second type of reaction might result from the sparking of her curiosity and an alerting of that portion of her femininity which requires her to test her attractiveness. She will begin to wonder how he managed to control himself and will embark on a series of truly feminine maneuvers which will bring her the reassuring answer to the question of her power, and this bed will truly flourish.

The intriguing variability inherent in humanity requires that all approaches be adaptable and that routine not be allowed to dominate.

I will long remember the patient who had been beating around the bush in embarrassment and finally blurted out, "Doctor, he drives me insane." I don't know how I managed to translate it so quickly, but I recognized what she meant immediately. Her arousal time was fairly rapid, and yet her husband insisted on going through a routine "warming" and "drove her to distraction."

This woman's role was one of aggressive femininity. She should have been more assertive in letting him know what she liked and what she wanted, and still remain feminine in the methods she used to inform him. When his hand progressed from one stage to the next, or from one zone to the next, she could move it back. If he lingered too long, she could move him on. When he neglected one part of the body, she could guide his hand to the forgotten area. She can be aggressive in allowing her body to speak. Certain pelvic movements are automatic, and all she needs to do is to let herself go. Above all, she can learn to cooperate.

Not all husbands are clumsy and brutal oafs. Some wives lock their knees together so rigidly that very little choice is left. Cooperate, and if you don't want to, help him understand why. Nature is of some help in that there are certain physical changes which occur in the female body that inform a husband as to the state of reaction. The nipple of the breast is a highly erogenous zone, and it contains some erectile tissue, so he can tell how much progress is being made. The body has its own language, and such things as pelvic movements, the staring glaze in the eyes, the swelling which occurs in the nasal passages making the breathing become louder, the change in respiratory rate, the flush that appears in the face are physical signs and changes that operate beyond conscious control.

The alert husband who has grown the antennae of sensitivity mentioned earlier learns to take all this in subconsciously and to utilize such information without becoming overly clinical or technical. Fortunately, the human mind is a tremendously capable organ. It can operate on many levels at once and still manage to let the left hand know what the right is doing.

In later years, as noted previously, the wife tends to respond more quickly as her sexual development progresses, and this requires certain adjustments. It is fundamentally true that foreplay is supposed to prepare the body for penetration of the vagina, and the intromission stage is to produce the culmination of procreation and orgasm. If response is coming more readily, the period of foreplay can be shortened and the stage of intromission thereby lengthened.

Diminishing the length of foreplay has an advantage for the male in that it increases his capacity to delay his orgasm, since his attempts to stimulate his wife have the effect of arousing him to a high pitch. By increasing the duration of this second stage, female orgasm can be produced more frequently and with greater intensity. As was noted, while the male is engaging in foreplay, he is subject to the most intense sexual stimulation. After all, he is capable of rapid arousal from fantasy alone, and when he is confronted with the object of his love and desire in the flesh, he is subject to the most exquisite pressure. It is little wonder that he often breaks under the strain and is practically driven to the completion of the act.

The couple's ability to handle this type of situation is a part of marital adjusting, and it is enhanced by their love and concern for each other. The male is able to delay his reaction by occasional pauses or stops. This applies to the period of vaginal penetration as well as the time of foreplay. Too often he makes the mistake of losing communication once penetration occurs, and his wife's reaction is one of loss. She feels deserted, because she is much more interested in him than in what he is doing. Perhaps it would be better expressed if we said she is interested only in what is done to her, and often she is not too certain that it is her down there. During one of these pauses the ears, the neck and the mouth can be kissed. Whispers of love can be pressed into her ear. While this is going on, movement is resumed, slowly and lightly at first. Finally, it bursts forth in the fullness of its power, and, hopefully, it carries her along with it to her climax at almost the same time as his. It is important that he watch his position during these phases so that he does not allow all of his weight to bear down on her pelvis and immobilize her.

As time passes and the early inhibitions of marriage are lost, and as the newness of things wear off, the need for variety and experimentation is brought up, usually by the man. The actual position the couple use for coitus is limited only by the imagination and the couple's athletic or acrobatic activity. She must be willing to cooperate in trying new approaches, and must not let herself be stopped by prejudice or by other people's opinion. Ideas that such things as the approach from the rear, or a position with the woman above, or sitting up in a chair, or what have you, are immoral and stupid are puritanical and harmful. What really is immoral is to be given an incomparable gift by the Lord and not learn how to use and enjoy it. The same feelings should apply to variations in foreplay, such as the male kissing the female genitals, or any other form of stimulation. The point at issue is not a problem of good or bad, but whether or not it is acceptable and enjoyable to both parties. If it is, then it is good and useful. If it isn't, why bother? When one partner—and this is usually the male—insists on promoting an activity that is distasteful and repulsive to the other partner, we are not dealing with a sexual problem in itself but with one complicated by personality disorders.

Before leaving this immediate subject, we should bring up the matter of signals. A description of body changes has been given, and it has been pointed out that these are signs which tell us what is happening, even when verbally denied. But certain private signals can be developed and used to avoid the need for words. A wife can often indicate her readiness for penetration by the way she handles the male organs—and the use of such sex play can often be used as an indication of readiness. As pointed out earlier, the feminine side is often most practical. When fully aroused, she may issue direct and rather startling instructions. This again is a highly personalized zone, and I am merely offering what some have used to facilitate their relatedness.

How to say "No"

One final point is the necessity for the woman to learn to say "no" to an aroused man without hurting him and without starting a second attack on her defenses. This, of course, first starts in the dating years when she is trying to control his over-aggressive lovemaking. It is assumed that she is in love with him, so she does not want to use such techniques as the lighted cigarette ground into the hand that wanders too far—accidentally, of course. All the conversational gambits have failed, so what is left? I call it the "down-boy-down" routine. It is based on a firm "no" accompanied by appropriate body defense maneuvers, and a kiss with a stranglehold on the neck. It is "no"—with love. Once the moment of crisis begins to subside, she can explain her reasons and try to make him understand. It must never be used unless she really means it. In other words, this should not at any time be a part of the, "No, but I really don't mean no", game. Once it is used there can be no retreat from the position taken—I love you, but. . . . Properly developed with its variations, it can be used all through marriage when it may be necessary to refuse intercourse, and it can be invaluable in the amount of hurt feelings and edgy tempers that can be prevented. Our aggressive male is, fortunately, built to absorb rebuff and bounce back, but there is no harm in making it easier on him.

When the female partner reaches the advanced stage of sexual growth, she may become more assertive and initiate action on her own. This is pleasing to the male most of the time, but it is possible he may refuse her, or merely lack enthusiasm. Look out! A woman scorned is a fearsome thing! Apparently her fear of abandonment, of desertion, her need for security, all rise up within her; and she doesn't take refusal well. Most men have seen this only once or twice, but they make sure it never happens again; or, if it does, they find a way to ease the fall and avoid the shock.

The ability to say "no" with love to a man and to maintain the negative, still easing out of this naturally tense situation gracefully, is one of those acts that requires the essence of true humaneness. It is difficult to describe, because it requires being two things at the same time. It is like trying to tell parents how to deprive a child of an attractive, but dangerous, object without making the child cry. It is difficult to instruct someone, because the description must go first to one view and then to another, first to the "no" and then to the love; but the action must be all in one piece. It is so easy to fall back on simple advice such as "love finds a way," "time will heal," and so forth. But the problem is now; the girl on a date wants to hold the boy, but she doesn't want to give in. The wife wants to put him off now but still would like to show her love and concern. I cannot offer her much more help than I can the mother whose child wants to play with a sharp knife. Stop him, love him and try to explain, but be careful. He will not listen except to pick out the parts of your explanation he can twist to his own use. During the dating period many of these conflicts can be handled only by breaking off the relationship, since the boy's objective is solely biological. But in marriage, of course, this is not desirable. Fortunately, the wife has many advantages in that a little extra care with her appearance and her cooking the next morning tells him a great deal more than hours of conversation.

To recapitulate, sexual life and growth can be compared to spiritual development in the sense that both take time and effort and come to various people in different degrees. All do not reach the same levels of success. Many marriages are sexual failures; and often, despite this, they are good, solid, functioning social units that bring great satisfaction and happiness to the couple and their children. I suspect this happens because the couple are honest enough to recognize and admit their failure. For far too many others the wife is labelled frigid, or the husband called incompetent, and the couple sink deeper and deeper into conflict, producing trouble for themselves and often for their children. In many of these cases the woman has been unable to achieve any sexual growth, and the marriage falls into a pattern dictated by the male-centered sexuality. For these people sex is a dirty word.

In the last fifty years more research and thinking have been directed toward the woman's role, and gradually a concept is arising which recognizes an equality of status without a sameness of persons. There is one male and one female, as different as night and day. Each possesses an equal share in the union that is marriage. Sexually, she is as important as he is; she is as unique in her individual sexuality as he is in his. Her participation should be as strong and as full as his but in a different and completely feminine manner. She becomes involved in the fullness of her womanhood.

To quote Dr. Marion Hilliard, author of *A Woman Doctor Looks at Love and Life,* "It is a relationship potentially as lovely and as lethal as a rope bridge over a chasm; it is capable of exalted beauty or sour doom. And, contrary to popular opinion, it is the woman and not the man who determines whether the act of love will enrich her life or curse it."*

For the woman, orgasm practically never occurs in the beginning of a marriage, but only after months or years. In too many cases orgasm does not occur at all. She must be allowed to grow into her sexuality. Such growth occurs only in an atmosphere of total involvement and love. We are not yet at the point of fully understanding this process, but in marriage counseling and in the practice of medicine, we see the need for love time and time again. As we extend the practice of medicine into personal and total care, we improve our communication with patients. They, in turn, give us the privilege of learning more about their personal relations in the marriage union. Patient after patient has expressed herself about the nature of the changes which occurred at a specific point in the marriage—at six months, at two years, or in the one

*Dr. Marion Hilliard, *A Woman Doctor Looks at Love and Life* (New York: Doubleday & Co., Inc., 1957).

dramatic case cited earlier, after eighteen years. They have been very honest in their comments as to how this has changed their attitude toward their children, toward their marriage, or toward their husband. Sex is no longer spoken of as a woman's burden; it becomes a glorious gift from their creator. Sex makes them truly two in one flesh and one mind.

I don't know of any way of describing the totality of the union so achieved. I can vividly remember talking to groups of married couples on the subject and noting the glow on the faces of some, while far too many others remained dull and uncomprehending. This type of union is seen only in marriage, or a marriage-like situation, because to grow into this situation the woman must have the security of total commitment on the part of the man; and she must have love in its fullest, spiritual sense. Love means continence on the part of the man when it is required. Love means that any element of force, and this includes duty, interferes with her capacity to respond. Love is a continual courtship on the part of the husband, because each act of intercourse is, in a sense, a remarriage; and the pleasures therein often outdo the honeymoon's.

The restrictions on sexuality imposed by charity in cases of illness, nervous fatigue, etc., are not only rules to live by; they are an essential part of the relationship. True married sexuality is a full-time occupation, not in the obsession of desire, but in the total involvement of persons. You cannot divide man and talk of his higher or lower natures, because this is a perversion of what he is. If a man wants to behave as an animal, he may do so; but in doing so, he changes and becomes an animal with all of an animal's limitations. He cannot be both human and animal. Sex for the human is truly an act of love which not only communicates this love, but becomes an essential part of it for the married person. Marriage can and does exist without sex but only in a crippled form, and only because intense effort is exerted to compensate for the failure. Marriage without sex is not the ideal the creator intended. It would certainly be perverse to have created something as powerful as the attraction of sex and not make it capable of lasting a lifetime. For various reasons, many loving people fail in sexual growth, but we should never deceive ourselves that such marriages are as good as those in which such growth is complete. The sexual bond, the joy and pleasure which is its essence, is the cement given to us to provide strength and security for marriage. Those millions of couples who have created secure marriages without this should be honored for their devotion but not taken as models for good marriages.

Sex for the woman is a part of her total life and not a separate compartment; so coitus is not an isolated incident in a day's activities, but an integral part of her life. In other words, the male who is thinking of having relations with his wife must be careful in all his activities. He must be conscious of the fact that he is trying to establish a mood and act accordingly. He cannot ignore her for long periods and then expect her to respond immediately. He maintains contact by listening when she talks, by calling her when he is absent, by touching her when he passes by, kissing her when there is no reason for kissing, and by telling her often how much he loves her. Perhaps the whole meaning can be covered in a short sentence. Every act of intercourse is an act of courtship. You do not own her. If you have any rights, they are worthless unless they are exercised in a loving atmosphere; so when you want her, win her! The good Lord gave you imagination and humor, and love gives you a light heart. Put them all together, and courtship will never become boring. Her response is easily worth the effort. Sexual development, when given the proper place to grow, helps to fulfill what many consider the primary purpose of human marriage, the achievement of union between two people. This is a merging which is at once mystical and physical; a two in one flesh which creates something new—a couple. From this union children come into a tiny world of love and security, a family.

4 Problems brought into the marriage

> ... she had never realized any love save love as passion. Such love though it expands itself in generosity and thoughtfulness, though it give to visions and great poetry, remains among the sharpest expressions of self-interest. Not until it has passed through a long servitude, through its own self-hatred, through mockery, through great doubts; can it take its place among the loyalties. Many who had spent a lifetime in it can tell us less of love than a child that lost a dog yesterday.
>
> —*Thornton Wilder*, The Bridge of San Luis Rey

Mental health

People say that sex does not *create* problems in marriage; it brings problems to a head. It is in the sexual phase of marriage that personality conflicts or tensions first start to cause trouble. Because this is true, it is difficult to avoid a discussion of psychiatry in regard to marriage problems. So much has been written on this element of humanity's knowledge about itself, and so many interpretations are offered that one hesitates to write about it; but it is impossible to avoid discussion of mental health in marriage.

As a person progresses from birth through infancy, childhood and adolescence to maturity, he acquires experiences and
knowledge of millions of things; and he experiences thousands
of emotional events of varying intensity. Each of these experiences leaves a mark, some small, others large. Some are isolated;
others are cumulative. Some are counterbalanced by opposite
events or emotions; others are reinforced.

Each of us started with a complex and unique genetic blueprint. The sum of our experiences acting on the blueprint, plus
our own interpretation and integration of each experience,
produces the individual—what I am; what you are. When we
marry, we bring into the union the sum of all the experiences
that have acted upon our unique personality, and the success
or failure of our interpretation and integration of these events
will influence the success or failure of our marriage.

One of the few axioms that can be applied to marriage is
that any difficulties carried by the individuals into the contract
will certainly not be improved by the marriage. They will
probably become worse. Nervous tension, inadequate preparation, ignorance, or any other of the ills that mankind is heir
to, will grow worse in marriage and will compound the natural
difficulty that any two people find in learning to live together.
The problems of society around us impinge on each one of
us as persons, and it is blindness not to see how this adds to
the burden we bring into matrimony.

The problems of our society, added to the personal problems of the married couple, sometimes impose an intolerable
burden on man and wife. And in eighty-five percent of marriages, one other person is also involved—the child of their
union. Very few children can survive a problem environment
without showing some effects of the tensions.

I am fully convinced that a hundred years from now scholars

in the behavioral sciences will wonder how any of us survived some of the terrible and traumatic things that are happening to children throughout our nation. The human organism has a fantastic ability to maintain homeostasis, but the price exacted from some is a terrible and a disfiguring one that can scar the individual for life.

I remember once stopping a psychiatrist friend of mine to comment on the lack of progress one of my patients was making. On this particular day he was unusually tired, and he sadly commented, "I am afraid nothing is going to help that poor woman except to put her back in the womb and start all over again."

Hers was a severe case of mental illness. To most of us, the words "mental illness" carry an explosive meaning. We automatically picture the fully psychotic individual raving mad, or staring wildly at a blank wall. Perhaps it is some primitive fear within our social memory that leads us to make this interpretation. But we should push away from our minds this medieval concept of despair when we speak of mental illness.

There are many varieties of mental illness, ranging all the way from a severe, incurable condition requiring commitment, to a simple personality quirk like the compulsion to keep every ashtray empty at all times.

Karl Menninger's description of mental illness as personality dysfunction and living impairment in which the patients are human beings obliged to make awkward and expensive maneuvers to maintain themselves is excellent. There are individuals who have become somewhat isolated from their fellows, harassed by faulty techniques of living, uncomfortable with themselves and often with others. Their reactions are intended to make the best of a bad situation and to forestall a worse one.

In other words, they want to insure survival, even at the cost of suffering and social disaster.

The "battered child" syndrome

To understand what this psychiatric gobbledygook means, one must take a long, hard look at childhood. We need not look at our own childhood, or the childhood of any of our friends. We should think about the growing years of *all* children. For some, childhood is a terrible, disastrous, even deadly experience. You have read newspaper accounts of children who were beaten severely; some have been murdered for some childish prank.

It is safe to assume that for every child who dies from one of these beatings there are thousands who survive physically. This has been publicized recently as the "battered child syndrome." Quite by accident some hospitals discovered that some children, brought in with fractures supposedly received by falling down the stairs, showed X-ray evidence of other fractures in various stages of healing.

Once alerted, medical authorities began to survey all injuries of certain types for evidence of previous damage. In a relatively short time two or three hundred cases were collected, some with a fantastic accumulation of physical trauma.

Psychiatric investigation of the parents usually brought out the story, and a picture of almost naked aggression was developed. Along with these reports of physical abuse, there are many cases of incest. Don't pass this off as applicable only to low social and economic classes. I have had five women patients from good middle class backgrounds who admitted that incestuous relations with their father was the reason for their failure to develop an orgasm with their husband. Various child psychiatrists have pointed out that more children are sexually abused in their own homes by members of the family than by the more notorious strange man on the street.

Now let's move into the more subtle forms of aggression. One example of this type of covert aggression is the mother who nags her children so much that they become depressed. I am thinking of the young child whose mother screams at her: "Eat, eat, eat!"

Later, the child walks to school with her head hanging and her whole body drooping like a wilted flower. You wonder whether her teacher will scold her for inattention, when she is crying inside, because she thinks her mother does not love her.

Later on, you meet the mother who, because she knows that you are a doctor, pours out her concern about her child who is so thin. You see the tension and worry in her eyes, and you try to reassure her. You try to convince her that children do grow up if they are allowed to proceed at their own pace. But you are afraid that your advice is not registering, because this mother is too tense and worried to listen to your plea for patience.

More harm has been done to children and to the adults they will become in the guise of helping them than the child beaters have ever done. The problem stems from a devilish twist in the human makeup called the unconscious mind. Much of what passes as concern for the child's welfare is unconscious aggression: the "I'm punishing you for your own good" syndrome.

Common sense tells us that some discipline is necessary, or life would become intolerable for everyone. But we must be sure that the discipline is really motivated by love, not by some unconscious striving for revenge, or for some other satisfaction. This is the heart of the puzzle.

The unconscious and the subconscious

Freud, like any innovator, made many mistakes. Quite a few of his theories are outdated, or have been modified; but his discovery of the unconscious will rank him among the giants for all time. He began with the premise that nothing is ever forgotten; it is just tucked away beyond recall for the present. Some memories are suppressed, swept under the rug, because we don't want them out in full view. These memories are often beyond recall, too. Finally, there are those memories that are so frightful, or frightening, that repression and loss of memory are automatic. Suppression is instinctive and almost immediate.

There would be no problem if such memories were pushed aside, and our life stream was allowed to continue undisturbed, but this doesn't happen. We constantly make associations, so that a comparatively innocent word, event or happening can trigger a reaction the intensity of which is due to the emotional burden of the original event or experience. Perhaps the following case history will illustrate the mechanism better than any description. This is not one of my own cases. It was related to me by the hypnotist who worked on the case with a university psychiatry department.

An unmarried woman of about fifty-five suffered from a rather unusual complaint, and it was making her life miserable. Whenever she saw a dog, she became incontinent (urinated spontaneously). No matter where she was or how she was dressed, this would happen. As a result, her life was extremely restricted. She was afraid to go out at all. Various psychotherapeutic procedures had failed to reveal any cause for this, so it was decided to try hypnotic regression. Under hypnosis, the patient was told that it was her fifteenth birthday, and she was able to describe the day in complete detail (no memory is ever really lost). Proceeding with this technique, it was found that the condition existed on her twelfth birthday, but not her eleventh. Continued exploration of this time period under hypnosis brought out her story about coming home from school late one day. She took a shortcut through an alley. On making a turn around a building, she ran into a man in the act of raping a woman. He grabbed the little girl by the neck and pressed a knife against her throat saying, "If you ever tell anyone about this, I'll kill you." She ran home crying but never told anyone.

Obviously, she urinated from fright. A dog may have been nearby in the alley to provide the trigger to provoke the reaction later in life. Note that the reaction was not associated with fear, and that she was not particularly frightened of dogs. These are protective mechanisms, after all.

When she woke up from the trance, she had no memory of what she had described. She even refused to believe the doctor when he repeated it. When the doctor played a tape recording of her voice under hypnosis, she was able consciously to recall the event.

Then it came out, with all the panic and hysteria compounded by the years of repression. It was necessary to hospitalize her, keep her under tranquilizers for many days, and wait for the hysteria to subside.

One of my own cases also illustrates what repressed fears can do to a person. Some years ago a patient about thirty-four with three children, an excellent husband and a generally satisfactory life, found that she was becoming more and more anxious month after month. By the time I first saw her, other doctors had tried tranquilizers with only temporary benefit. She was severely agitated, and as she talked she became almost hysterical.

Most of her trouble seemed to date from the time her eighty-two-year-old father had moved in with them. As I directed her conversation into her relations with her husband, it soon became obvious that things were seriously wrong. When she tried to talk about this, her mind wandered. Once or twice she developed an almost psychotic stare and broke into wild changes of subject, including some dark hints about myself and some of my patients.

I was seriously considering the diagnosis of an early psychosis when the husband paid me a visit. He was concerned, because his wife seemed to be getting much worse, but her behavior at home revealed none of the traits I had seen. The behavior he described was more in the realm of pure anxiety. I explained that this change was probably due to our sessions, and I promised that I would refer her to a psychiatrist, if I thought it would help. I also told him that we seemed to be making progress.

On her next visit I steered the conversation to her father's presence in the house, and the effect this was having on her marital relations with her husband. She denied any problem here, because her father was always out at a neighborhood tavern. Besides, his room was far from hers, so his presence in her home did not bother her.

Once we were on the subject of her father it was simple to shift to her childhood. Soon a picture emerged of an old-fashioned father from an Eastern European culture who completely dominated a quiet mother and harshly ruled his only daughter, who was very attractive. When she was about eleven she accidentally met a male schoolmate on the way to a Sunday matinee. The boy asked to go along with her, and she agreed. On the way home they stopped for a milkshake, and she arrived late for supper. Supper was eaten in stony silence, and immediately afterward her two brothers were sent to their rooms, and the third degree began. She tried to lie, but in her panic she made too many mistakes. Finally the boy's name slipped out and then the whole story.

The father exploded with wrath, tore off all her clothes and chased her around the house, whipping her with his leather belt and loudly bellowing torrents of foul words. All this time her mother was screaming ineffectively and getting knocked down for interfering.

After the patient calmed down, she admitted that she and her husband had achieved excellent sexual rapport, which she enjoyed more each year, and that both he and she enjoyed nudity in the bedroom. Since her father had moved in, she had found herself unable to relax with her husband and had become unresponsive to intercourse. She admitted that this created tension between her and her husband, and that this, in turn, made her more anxious and frightened that she might lose her husband.

We continued our discussion for a few more sessions, and she gradually realized that one could hate some things a stupid father had done, and yet love an old man who drank a little too much and was very lonely for his poor, quiet little wife who had died five years ago. I also recommended that, at least temporarily, she and her husband forego the pleasure of their usual free love play. By remaining somewhat covered, she could be more tolerant. This proved to be true, and we had no more sessions.

She wrote about two months later stating that everything

was improving. She had even talked back to her father occasionally. She also said that the relapses I warned her about were coming farther and farther apart. There also was a pleasant note from the husband, adding his thanks for what I had done.

Now, admittedly, this is one of those dramatic cases with a classic, specific injury or trauma to which troubles can be traced; but it does illustrate how something that happens at the age of eleven lies dormant and then erupts at the age of thirty-four to cause trouble. Ofter the cause is not apparent during the eruption, and it might remain hidden without a great deal of luck or some help from a trained outsider.

A great number of cases apparently do not have a single dramatic childhood trauma such as this. It is more likely that they are made up of years and years of little troubles, which are much more difficult to recall, and hence more difficult to understand.

The burden produced by the isolation of the individual in modern society makes all efforts to strengthen marriage more crucial as the years pass.

Marriage courses and sex education

Unless corrective measures are instituted, marriage is likely to have more troubles at an ever-compounding rate. Unless individual problems can be solved early, more bad marriages will result. These marriages will produce tension-ridden offspring, who will also enter difficult marriages.

Every effort we can exert to help people choose marriage partners more carefully, to enter into marriage with more adequate preparation, and to provide education that will help people form happy and productive marriages, will be repaid tenfold in the future improvement of our people and our society. Adequate sex instruction and increased knowledge provided by honest research on the subject will benefit all of us in more healthy unions and a more vigorous society.

We must take a long view of this sex education, since this is life itself, and life is long and getting longer. I have stated previously, and I will repeat frequently my firm belief that sex education really belongs in the home. In truth, most sex education is given in the home, whether the parents like it or not. Even if the word "sex" is never spoken, and the subject scarcely mentioned, the education is carried out in the relations of father to mother, mother to son, father to daughter, brother to sister, and so on. Sex education is, to a great extent, sensed and felt through the sensitive emotional antennae of a child. After all, sex is either maleness or femaleness, and this is rather difficult to hide and hard to avoid. Silence can be louder than words; a look can be more expressive than a speech. It is by these means that a child absorbs the feelings and emotions which are the basis of our concern. The more academic or formal sex education in schools and books is often remedial to supplement what was not given, or to undo faulty instruction. In this day and age no parent can hope to bring up a child in silence or ignorance. There are too many other sources of information. One cannot hope to impose standards of continence on the male, or premarital chastity on the female by edict alone.

We must speak to the young on the levels where they are listening. When articles appear recommending sexual freedom as a means of developing personality, we must talk about what happens to the followers of such a policy. We want freedom of discussion; we must have discussion, not silence. If the young people want to talk about a problem, we must help them reach their own solutions. Our solutions in the past haven't always been good. Some of them know this only too well from their own lives, because they are a part of our marriages. The people most deeply affected by a marriage may very well be the children.

Sexual relations between husband and wife have an effect on the children beyond initiating their existence. One of our most ridiculous errors in the past was our belief that we could hide things from children. Growing things have a sensitivity. They live in an atmosphere, a milieu. For human beings this includes the world of emotion, of sensations beyond definition, of feeling and of reward and punishment.

Sex with love is one of the greatest unifiers, compounders, and bringers-together there is in our big and lovely world. The looks, the touching of fingertips, the smiles exchanged between married lovers are beautiful. That all the world loves a lover is a trite and shopworn statement; but a happily married couple is a special joy and a sustenance to their children. One of the primary factors in reaching this state is through and with sexual union, not because sex is so important, but because it is so uniquely human, and because so many other attributes must be developed if it is to succeed. So I do not think I am making too big a jump when I point out that the parents' intercourse when the child is five years old might be almost as important to the child as the act of coitus in which he was originally conceived.

A factor concerning parental conflict that is too often ignored is that the child often feels he or she is the cause of the trouble between the parents. Remember, a child is egocentric. He feels that the world revolves around him. When loud voices and louder silences fill the home, the youngster's first thought often is, "What did I do to make daddy so mad?"

All too often, in the careless cruelty of the argument, the child will be used by one parent against the other. He may shout, "Why can't you keep the brat quiet?"

She will complain, "Why do I have to be stuck with these damn kids all day?"

Guilt so engendered can grow and fester with time until it overwhelms a child.

Now I cannot claim that all sexually-responsive marriages are happy; but such couples usually become more closely united, because sex becomes better as the years of marriage pass and greater communication is established. Quarrels always occur, but the long silences, which seem worse to the child than a fight, become shorter, and making up becomes easier and more lasting.

The thing we are seeking as parents is to teach the child the meaning of love. This is what changes sex into sexuality and makes sexual intercourse a joy to a man and a woman for all of their lives. Love, of course, can never be taught. The child learns about love as he or she lives in love. It grows as the child watches the parents treat each other with affection. You can see it in your own child's face when your fifteen-year-old daughter catches you kissing your wife in the kitchen and teases you about no necking being allowed, or tells you to watch out for that body contact. All the time her eyes are really all aglow with love for you, herself and all life. Your boys are a little quieter and sometimes a little stuffy, but don't worry. They feel the same way, but just can't show it until they find a girl of their own.

I am not asking for exhibitionism; that only embarrasses children. I am thinking about love that overflows into little acts. This tone sets the style of all sex instruction so that explanations of the things mommies and daddies do have a validity that is easily recognized by children. Children have an uncompromising honesty and an extremely accurate sense of the validity of things. This is the reason why the state of their parents' marriage is so important to them; and this is the reason why preparation for marriage and efforts to make marriage succeed are so very important. References to love are meaningless when they come from parents in a chronically dissonant marriage.

This discussion of childhood influences and unconscious memories is just a preface to a discussion about emotional problems that one or both partners can bring into a marriage without being aware of their existence. Problems such as aggressive sexuality, promiscuous behavior, homosexuality, frigidity and impotence can all be traced to influences reaching back into time before the marriage. The reactions can be out of proportion to the present difficulty, as explained earlier; and, of course, the reactions cannot be explained or understood in terms of the current situation alone.

This is not a claim for determinism, nor does it give anyone an excuse for various forms of misbehavior. It is merely an attempt to explain some of the sources for trouble in marriage and to alert couples to the need for professional help when their own efforts produce no improvement.

Don Juan

These problems can invade the sexual realm even when sex education has been excellent and general sexual functioning quite normal. Other aspects of emotional development may be a problem, and sexuality may be used in an attempt to cope with the original difficulty. As an example, the Don Juan may use sex purely to bolster his prestige and compensate for inner feelings of masculine inadequacy. An insecure, grasping girl may use sex for "gold digging."

What is meant by inner feelings of masculine inadequacy? It means that the man has not developed an image of himself as a man that satisfies what he expects of himself. Part of our trouble is that we men still live in our ancient past when we were the hunters, the protectors and the providers. We often get the feeling that we are in prison, that we are being trapped; and we yearn for the old days when men were men. We have difficulty reconciling the sedentary present with the old image of man as the hunter. We cannot reconcile the cry for equal rights for women with the age-old image of the male as a provider. Female teachers and female-oriented education, plus the absent father, promote the feeling of masculine inadequacy. An old human trick for overcoming a defect is to overcompensate, to come back stronger to make up for lost time.

The more inadequate Don Juan feels, the more aggressive his sexual behavior becomes. By involving himself with multiple partners, he bolsters his ego as a superior male. He often succeeds for quite a long while. Then the whole façade crumbles, and a pathetic, torn figure of a man ends up in a psychoanalyst's office.

What happens if he marries? Often he will choose a nice, "untouchable" girl, because she is a challenge, or because he is tired of all these "bad" women. Don Juan is really a puritan at heart. He may have tried to maintain his masculine image by conquering "inferior" women, but he marries an ideal woman, a woman on a pedestal, a mother-image.

After he has married, his ego begins to droop, because he feels he cannot make any more conquests. When he attempts to restore his ego by cheating, he introduces conflict and turmoil into his marriage. If his wife develops any sexual response, it upsets him, because "mothers" are not supposed to be sexy. This problem would not be so difficult to solve if Don Juan and his wife understood the cause. But the trouble is masked by complicated rationalizations and self-deceit. A professional counselor may have to work very hard and listen many hours before he can detect the sources of the problem.

All of us have trouble communicating. That is why the word itself has become popular and has replaced the older word, "speaking." We have learned that communicating is more than words. It includes looks, tone of voice, volume of voice, posture of body and innumerable other actions, which are clues to thoughts and feelings. When a person suffers emotional disturbance of any duration or intensity, his words may mean the opposite of what he says. To avoid the really painful area, he focuses his attention on something else.

We also must look at our man's partners, the premarital and extramarital partners in his affairs, and the one he chooses in marriage, his wife. If he is running around in an attempt to bolster his masculinity, what about the women who cater to him? In most cases these women are trying to use sex to solve a serious personal problem. Their childhood was devoid of, or sorely lacking in, love, and the religious barriers against premarital intercourse have weakened. So they capitulate, because this brings them close to another human being.

This can produce an overwhelming reaction, which may actually develop a type of orgasm, or it may satisfy because of the emotional intensity. Unfortunately, the partner doesn't respond to this. He is looking for sexual relief and actually despises this "inferior" woman. Such a relationship is temporary and strictly follows the old adage of "love 'em and leave 'em." Women are extremely resilient and capable of rapid recovery so that they apparently go through the same

rather horrifying experience of love-ecstasy-pain in rather
rapid order. This reaction is so prevalent that many writers
think promiscuous women are basically masochistic. Sooner
or later they manage to trap some male into marriage, and so
they concentrate their troubles under one roof.

The promiscuous male sometimes abuses his "inferior"
partner. More than one girl has been wined, dined and treated
like a queen by a soft-spoken, well-to-do, refined man during
the seduction, only to find that this "gentleman" will beat her
up like a trollop to terminate the affair. Neither one of the
parties is likely to brag about this aspect of the play boy world.

Women are going through their crisis, too. They have all
of their childhood problems remaining with them, plus the
load of inhibitions placed by those foolish people who still
think ignorance is innocence. Despite our modern liberality,
far too many girls are totally ignorant of their own reproductive anatomy, are ashamed of it and incapable of doing what
nature requires them to do.

The introduction of sex education in schools, starting in
kindergarten, will help to change this, but more help is needed
from parents. In case your hair bristled at the mention of sex
education in lower grade school, let me point out exactly what
it means. The curriculum outline below, in very sketchy form,
should speak for itself:

I Respecting the privacy and rights of others
    A. Separate use of bathroom
    B. Proper habits of washing, etc.—privacy a normal wish, not
       an expression of shame
    C. Private parts of the body are just private, not shameful
II Childhood safety in going to and from school
    A. Instil attitude of caution
    B. Make effort to avoid general distrust of all persons

III Attitude toward family life
   A. Mother-father roles; husband-wife
   B. Constant reference to mother, father, husband, wife and not men and women is called "halo effect"
   C. Child's attitude toward new baby
IV Animals in class
   A. Growth
   B. Development

In grades two to four, body growth, fetal development, use of food, animal growth, feelings, emotions and relations with people are all developed to present a well-rounded background. In fifth grade, detailed reproductive anatomy is taken up along with the anatomy of the circulatory system, respiratory system, etc.

The whole purpose is to ground the child in reality so that dating problems and danger of venereal disease or pregnancy can be taken up with a family-centered approach. This will counter the information the young person is being exposed to in the streets, popular press and other sources, which are so open to them today.

The present crisis in femininity stems mainly from a woman's changing role in society. Her relations with her mother are almost as good as they were in past years. A daughter suffers from an absent father, but not, of course, in the same way her brother does. She is adversely affected by her contact with the inadequate male trying to prove his worth.

She is tempted on almost all her dates, and constant attempts are made to go as far as possible with her, so she cannot possibly fail to react. Young men will call her frigid if she tries to maintain any standards; and she is surrounded by a barrage of propaganda about the evils of repression and her need for free expression. She needs freedom from pressure and freedom to love in a tender and protected milieu. Don't try to tell her that frantic copulation in the back seat of a car, or one-night drinking bouts mixed with a few rounds of wrestling in a motel is freedom for her. This is not her kind of sex. It brings her nothing but an emotional hangover and loss of self-respect.

Few women have any grounds for pride in being able to bring the average man to bed. That is much too easy to be proud of. She cannot even rationalize it as he does. It's too easy to make a conquest out of it. Some women are able to do this, because for various reasons they utterly despise all men. They despise men so deeply that they use sex to make men squirm. Looking at the act of intercourse from the point of view of a totally disinterested female, even a man can recognize it as a pathetic and comic activity. Prostitutes are often prime examples of this type, and they are sometimes extremely expressive about what they think of their "tricks." Some of these girls are starved for love and affection, and they will pay the price of shame and desertion for even a relatively short and cheap imitation of the real thing.

The glamour girl

Another handicap that some women can bring into marriage is the glamour girl syndrome. Many workers in the marriage field have commented on glamour girl frigidity. This is the fantastically perverse picture of a woman, who is the epitome of sexual attraction. But she cannot react normally, despite some years of marriage, and despite a good measure of pre-marital experience. I have never seen an analysis of the reason for this aberration, but I can describe what some of my patients, who fall into this class, have said.

For one thing, they often feel as though they were two people. There is the "me" who is known by practically no one and liked by none. Then there is the "her," a person everyone notices. They talk about "her" in an unflattering way. They attribute sexiness to "her."

But the real person, the "me," is neither aggressive nor sexy. She is quiet, shy and anxiety-ridden. She can't bluff her way by assuming the cold, haughty look that her other half uses to fool everyone.

I certainly can't prove it, but I believe that these glamour girls encounter a great deal of impotence in marriage. The failing male marries a sex image in the hope that it will overcome his impotency by the intensity of the stimulation. Since impotence is almost always due to internal psychological troubles, the intensification of desire would make him worse, not better.

This deadly matching of one problem to another occurs more frequently than would seem possible. It is amazing how capable some sufferers are at picking just the person to make their situation worse. If they divorce, they walk right into the same situation again and again.

The glamour girl frigidity syndrome is not hard to understand if we remember that the man who marries her expects her to be sexy. He certainly will not spend much time and effort in loving her. Yet this is exactly what this lonely girl needs.

The gold digger

Finally, there is the gold digger who uses sex for gain. I have often referred to this as married prostitution. The evil ranges in intensity from the youngster who pets a little or a lot, in direct proportion to the amount of money the boy spends on the date, or the cost of the car he drives, to the married woman who withholds her favors when she fails to get what she wants and grants them when she does. When sex is used in this manner, how can it become the language of love?

A certain amount of teasing on the part of the woman is acceptable to herself and her husband, if she is clever enough to get away with it; but she usually does this out of love. He may be depressed with his job, everything else in his life may be falling apart and his ego may need a little building up. So she recognizes his need and offers him sympathy and gentle physical contact, mothering, if you want to call it that. He responds with an arousal pattern, and she may go along with him, even though her own feelings are mainly supportive and maternal. This type of intercourse is not repulsive to her. It is acceptable and even enjoyable, because she is doing something for the man she loves. Her husband may do the same thing for her when, despite fatigue and lack of desire, he works himself into the mood, because she feels lonely and the children have been more nerve-racking than usual. He gives her a shoulder to cry on. She does so, and his fatherly pats become more husbandly. A major difference is, of course, that he will react as completely in his orgasm as he would at any other time.

Impotence

The impotence which occurs on the wedding night or in the early months of marriage has already been discussed. It has been termed the impotence of inexperience. If accepted by both partners with equanimity and love, no problems arise. However, if the wife is antagonistic toward men for reasons that reach way back into her past, her suppressed antagonism may come to the surface as careless remarks that cut deeply into the wounded male psyche. This may set up a chain of disturbances which could become a problem. In a majority of cases the problem usually diminishes and disappears.

Many times a man may be impotent because he is afraid of hurting a girl, or because he cannot bear to see his loved ideal as a sexual partner. The latter reason is becoming more rare in our time. Some complications may also arise if there are marked feelings of guilt and fear about masturbation, particularly fear that masturbation had damaged the genital organs or function. If impotence at first coitus is added to these other fears, serious consequences may ensue.

Qualitative impotence is a puzzling phenomenon to most lay people and to many doctors. This means that the male is capable of sexual relations with one female and is impotent with another. The most common type occurs when the husband is impotent with his wife but not with a prostitute or with any other woman he considers inferior. In cases where impotence develops after a couple has been married for some years, a likely explanation is that the husband has repressed hatred for his wife. In such cases the male may use illness as an excuse. The illness may either be his own or his wife's. In situations where this condition exists from the beginning, or from the early years of marriage, I would assume it is due to a conflict in the man's mind about his mother, and the entire role of the wife in marriage. This type of man has categorized women as either the good, idealized, mother-image, or the bad, sexy, loose woman.

One of my patients told me about an interesting variation of this classification. Her husband became impotent when she became pregnant and recovered immediately after the delivery. In subsequent pregnancies this did not occur, although frequency of intercourse dropped considerably.

One of the complicating factors in these cases is that the wife begins to feel insecure, because she feels that her husband's indifference is due to her lack of sexual attraction. She may try to overcome this defect by dressing and acting more boldly. Naturally, this only makes the situation worse for the poor, mixed-up husband when his wife, the glorious mother, starts acting like a "loose" woman.

I have never seen it, but I have read reports of cases where the male becomes impotent when his wife is unresponsive. This has bothered the husbands of my patients, but I have no direct knowledge regarding actual cases of impotence. However, they could easily happen, since many women hesitate to acknowledge their own sexual inadequacy, let alone acknowledge that it is the reason for their husband's impotency.

Premature ejaculation has already been described as a normal occurrence in early marriage, but when it continues beyond the first few months it may be a variation of impotence. Impotence is devastating to the female partner, because she tends to blame herself, and because it may prevent her from becoming pregnant. But premature ejaculation is nerve-racking, because it creates partial stimulation, which rarely, if ever, leads to orgasmic fulfillment. Various techniques may prevent this from happening. One is to cut down on psychic stimulation by thinking of a golf game or something else, by tightening up the anal sphincter as hard as possible, or by careful use of cerebral depressants like alcohol.

Doctor Masters is supposed to have discovered from his work that the cremaster muscle which lifts the testicles up close to the body must be contracted before ejaculation can occur, so that, if the wife can hold the testicles down from the body, the male remains potent as long as she desires. I would hesitate recommending this for fear there might be some rather gruesome accidents. But people will experiment. If it is successful, I am sure the idea will catch on.

Some attempts to solve the problem may work for one man and have no benefit whatever for another. Trial and error is the only approach. Other methods are based on reducing the amount of vaginal friction as previously described. Some find that by changing coital position, such as side to side, or with the woman on top, orgasm can be delayed. Another means of prolonging the male's ability, or of his training himself to delay orgasm, is to learn to recognize the sensation of impending ejaculation. This is localized in the glans penis and corpus spongiosum. Movement and stimulation is then interrupted until the sensation subsides. Penile stimulation is then resumed and stopped again. This can be continued as long as possible, and gradually some can control the timing of orgasm, and release it when the wife has reached her premonitory level.

Frigidity in the woman is in some ways comparable to impotence in the male, but it is far more complex. At least the male is attempting to have coitus; but the frigid woman may often reject any attempt on the part of the male to initiate an arousal pattern. A common occurrence for her is uniquely female; for various psychological reasons, she can lose her response before she reaches orgasm, even though she is fully aroused. Although she and her husband do everything possible, she still may be unable to attain orgasm. This almost never occurs in the male, but this so-called orgasmic impotence is a common condition in the female. It is particularly frustrating to her in that she is brought to a high pitch of arousal and left suspended. She is introduced to all the joy of what this relationship can mean and then robbed of the culmination at the last moment.

Frigidity, like impotence, can be selective in nature, both as to situation and as to partner. Obviously, the female orgasm depends on the erective potency of the male and on his endurance or ability to prolong his ejaculation, plus his skill in approaching courting and lovemaking. Even a perfectly healthy woman cannot arrive at an orgasm when a man suffers from premature ejaculation, or any of the other problems noted above. As in the case of impotence, frigidity can be involved in a distortion of the woman's image of herself as a woman, her unhappiness with her role in life and her hidden hostility against the male sex. Add to these difficulties distortions in father-daughter relationships, and there is fertile ground for a good deal of trouble. When honest efforts repeatedly meet with failure, and ordinary counseling from doctor, clergy or social workers fails, any attempt to bring order into the psychology of frigidity will have to be left to a psychiatrist. Recognized family counseling centers can be very useful, because the better ones operate under psychiatric supervision. If counseling fails, psychiatric referral should be sought, but care should be taken that the psychiatrist is competent and is interested in this problem.

There are organic causes for frigidity and impotence, but they account for only a small percentage of the total number of cases. This would be a good place to point out that some of us bring physical weaknesses or handicaps into marriage, and others bring psychological defects. Those who have psychological defects may even be psychotic.

Mental illness
It is true that many psychological crises arise in marriage, but the roots of these crises are buried deep. When these defects

develop into mental illness, it is one of the most devastating and shocking things that can happen to anyone you know and particularly to someone you love. Too many times in my practice I have had the painful task of trying to make a husband realize what was happening to his wife, or of trying to make the wife see that the fights and bitterness she found directed at her were coming from a disordered and sick mind.

Not all psychotics fit into the common picture of the raving maniac who hears voices and sees visions. Some psychotics are only suffering changes in personality. A previously quiet, gracious husband becomes loud and vulgar, talks incessantly, and seems bursting with energy and ambition. The friendly wife becomes withdrawn, refuses to go out, no longer looks after herself or her children and goes into deep depressions.

Any severe change in personality, any rigidity of behavior that wasn't present before, any sudden appearance of very strong fears, should alert us that trouble may be brewing. The other partner should feel free to ask either her doctor or his for advice, particularly when the afflicted person is not under a doctor's care at the time. It is sometimes very difficult to get patients to obtain care, since they resent anyone questioning their "sanity."

Many well-meaning relatives shy away from these problems and advise doing nothing on the basis that illness will go away. Many of these conditions do come and go, improve and then get worse; but the general trend is always toward deterioration. Early diagnosis and treatment plus good family cooperation is extremely beneficial. Sometimes it will shorten the period of treatment appreciably.

When such a disaster does strike a marriage, I suggest that the partner not become involved in placing the husband or wife under hospital treatment. In cases where I have seen this done by husbands of my patients, the wives have harbored antagonism toward their husbands for "putting them away." This reaction may be due to our still primitive attitudes toward mental illness and may disappear as we become more understanding of this common type of illness; but since it interferes with the union of the couple, I believe it should be commented upon.

Alcoholism

Another very difficult condition that arises in marriage, but whose origins predate it by many years, is alcoholism. No condition I know about can be more disruptive and destructive to a marriage than alcoholism.

Descriptions of life with an alcoholic are really frightening. I can never forget the mother of three who told me she walked the streets in her nightgown almost every night her husband was home. She took her children with her, because her husband was so drunk that he was careening about the house with a loaded gun in his hand, threatening to shoot her, the children and himself. Anyone who reads the daily paper knows that this is no idle threat.

Then I recall a young mother with five children. Her oldest boy was twelve. Her husband came in one night, pulled her out of bed, stripped her clothes off, and then he dragged her screaming into the boy's room and threw her on the boy's bed with the shout, "There's your mother; she's a whore!"

Alcoholism is a terrible illness; and it has a terrible mental effect on many women, because they feel they are the cause of it. Because the disease, and it is a disease, is chronic, and because it usually exists for years in a hidden state, most marriages with alcoholics are unsuccessful sexually. Often the wife has labeled herself frigid, or she has been called so by her husband; so guilt and remorse are an integral part of the picture.

This is a complicated "game," in the sense in which Dr. Eric Berne uses the word. Although it involves many people, the main players are the alcoholic and the persecutor. The persecutor is the spouse of the alcoholic. In early stages, according to Dr. Berne, "the wife may play all three supporting roles: at midnight, the Patsy, undressing him, making him coffee and letting him beat up on her; in the morning, the Persecutor, berating him for the evil of his ways; and in the evening the Rescuer, pleading with him to change them."

The proper role to assume is that of an adult who is patient, understanding and firm. One should not be vindictive or punishing; but neither should one be tolerant of foolishness. The adult is constantly aware of a total situation, and he thinks of long-range goals, not of immediate gratification. The adult wife will not go to extremes to hide her husband's problems. If he falls into a drunken stupor on the front porch at two in the morning, she will call for help to get his 250 pounds inside the house, instead of injuring herself trying to carry him in without help, so that no one will find out that he is an alcoholic.

If the bottle brings him pain and misery, let it come. Don't rub it in, but never let him forget where the trouble comes from. Above all, get professional help as soon as you recognize his condition. Some of the worst situations I have ever seen are those marriages where the wife continues year after year in an absolutely impossible environment until she and the children are wrecks, all because she couldn't make the decision to break away and salvage what she could before it was too late. True alcoholics have only two ways to go: complete abstinence or utter ruin. There is no middle course. Some psychiatrists claim that the alcoholic is completely cured only when he is able to drink moderately again, but they admit that these cases are very, very rare. Most ex-alcoholics I know, even some who haven't touched a drop for twenty years, state that they are still alcoholics and will die alcoholics.

Obviously, sex and alcohol are incompatible. Frigidity or unresponsiveness for the wife is to be expected; and impotence for the male is frequent, because alcohol is a cerebral depressant, and because the alcoholic diet produces an assortment of diseases, many of them deadly to the total person, as well as to the reproductive system. Unfortunately, this comes late in the course of the disease; and too many pregnancies are an added problem for these wives.

The alcoholic wife is almost unknown, not because she doesn't exist (and in fairly large numbers) but because women alcoholics are more clever at hiding their problem. I once heard a female member of Alcoholics Anonymous describe the subterfuges she devised to hide her disease from her obstetrician during her pregnancy. He never found out; and I could see why, because I have been able to recognize so few alcoholics. Sexuality in the female alcoholic is horrible. Promiscuity, or even outright prostitution in marriage, is not unheard of. It should not be surprising to find out that alcohol is the explanation for some of the more lurid newspaper accounts of suburban scandals.

Homosexuality

Of all the problems brought into a marriage, one of the most shock-producing to the partner is the discovery that the mate of the opposite sex is homosexual. It may come as a surprise to some to find that male homosexuals get married to females, but this is one of the anomalies of human behavior.

One of the most tragic cases is that of the young bride of three months, extremely attractive, and in early pregnancy, whose apparently virile young husband announced that there will be no more children and no more sexual relations, because he is a homosexual.

I am not capable of explaining the psychological patterns of homosexuals, and I do not think I should attempt to evaluate their behavior in this book; but it does seem to me that many homosexuals attempt to cure themselves by exposure to female attractions. Perhaps they believe that marriage to a beautiful girl will bring out their latent manhood and overpower this quirk which is in them. The consequences are tragic for both, and especially unfortunate for this girl. She was a Catholic and unable to get permission to remarry. I believe that the changes implemented by Vatican II will make it possible to push a properly managed and documented case through the *Rota*, or church courts. Even under the present laws of the church, a wife could obtain an annulment, because the husband acted in bad faith if he married, knowing that he was a homosexual. Such a contract would not be valid.

We cannot be too critical of the church's attitude when so many of our better-educated people still think that the cure of the homosexual is a matter of will power. I wonder how many people told this poor young man that all he had to do was to try harder.

Other types of male homosexuality exist for years, because the person involved is capable of both homosexual and heterosexual relations. For some women the shock of learning that her husband is a homosexual may not come until she reaches middle age, and her husband is arrested for molesting young men or boys. The effect of this condition on sexual development in the marriage is disastrous. Unfortunately, the cure rate is very low even if the person is willing to make the effort.

Female homosexuality is an entirely different matter, since a woman is capable of allowing intercourse solely by an act of the will. Sexual response to the act is not needed at all. Lesbians can live in marriage for years and even fake responsiveness, if necessary, to maintain their "front." It even provides them with a field of operation, because it is perfectly normal for a housewife to go out with a woman friend or neighbor for hours at a time. Difficulties do arise, as they do in any double life; but many of her lapses are covered up with the husband's help, because he doesn't want exposure any more than she does.

Latent homosexuality refers to a person who has deep-seated tendencies in this direction, which are repressed. He or she functions on the surface as a normal heterosexual person, or even as an overly aggressive one. People so afflicted face insuperable problems in marriage, because they are torn by conflict. Since they are unaware of the source of the trouble, there is little they can do about it. Finally, the interpersonal difficulties of the marriage union become so overwhelming that professional help must be sought. This type of relationship can be unusually stormy and full of hostility.

The above histories and comments are included to demonstrate one of the reasons why sexuality can be difficult to understand, and why it is so compound and complex at times. These examples of conflicts in marriage may help us understand why we behave so unreasonably at times. All of us have done things that secretly surprised us. We wondered why we said that, or what prompted such an outburst of temper. It is not necessary to attempt any self-analysis. All we need is a little more tolerance for ourselves and for others, plus a little more respect for the wonderful, but sometimes frightening, human mind. Only when we find ourselves doing the same thing over and over, or catch ourselves falling into the same trap repeatedly, do we need to be concerned. If this is happening, and it it is seriously disrupting our lives, then we should ask for help.

The varied emotional content in sexuality, its delicacy and susceptibility to influence from a far-ranging variety of sources, should come as no surprise to any of us. After all, sex can be responsible for the most brutally sadistic murders as well as the most heroic renunciation and sacrifice. It can be seen in the most vulgar and debased forms and yet become man's greatest glory. If this is true, why should we be surprised when sex occasionally causes surprise and discomfiture in even the most stable of living patterns?

Perhaps this is why we need to have a firm grip on our attitude toward sexuality in marriage, what we expect from it and how we use it. We need a self-imposed party line, a developed sense of responsibility and concern, and a sense of humor, of toleration and of patience. Life is long and time heals. The young man is impatient, callous and aggressive; but twenty years later, when chided by his wife for turning to look at a pretty young girl, he may turn to her and say, "When I stop looking you can throw me out, because I'll be dead. If you think I could chase her and start all over again, you're crazy. Why should I spend twenty years helping her to grow to what you are now?"

Sexuality does have its infancy and its maturity, and the difference is an adhesive force that binds the couple in a unique companionship, a union that grows stronger year after year. Sometimes in marriage counseling work or premarriage education, we place so much attention on the problems; and we expend so much effort warning about impending difficulties, that we draw a morbid picture of marriage. Well, this is natural. When one is vitally concerned about love and beauty and wants others to share it, we know we must show both sides of the picture; but we try to emphasize the positive, attempt the beautiful. I hope that my basic attitude regarding the beauty, joy and sanctity of a good marriage will show in the following chapters.

Perhaps the following case history will give some idea of my point of view. When I was an intern, one of my duties was to pronounce a patient dead. No body could be transferred to the hospital morgue until we had performed an examination and certified that the person was really dead. One of my recurring fears was that I would make a mistake, and that one of my "patients" might wake up in the morgue. The hospital rumor-factories were full of such stories. Although I had never known of an authentic case, and still haven't to this day, I approached such situations with fear and trembling and with all my senses alerted. A gentleman who was eighty-six years old was on my service. He was very ill with pneumonia. His wife, who was eighty-two, occupied the room next to his as a "boarder."

This was many years ago when hospital costs were lower, and bed space was not so scarce; healthy people were often allowed to use the hospital as a hotel. I had seen them together many times, and I knew they had enjoyed a long and happy marriage, even though they had never had any children. During visiting hours large numbers of young people came to see them. It soon became apparent that they had been foster parents for most of the neighborhood children.

One night I received a call that his condition had worsened, and I went to his room. He had slipped into a coma, and he died shortly after I arrived. The nun who was working as night supervisor was with me. She was saying the prayers for the dying while I used the feeble measures available to us in this preantibiotic era. When it became obvious that we had lost him, we both suddenly remembered his wife sleeping next door; and debated with each other as to who would tell her. We finally compromised and both of us entered her room. As we opened the door and turned on the light, we found her lying peacefully and permanently asleep. Apparently she had passed away quietly in her sleep at about the time he did.

I have never been able to forget this couple who lived beyond their golden wedding day and passed away together, almost as though one could not live without the other. What kind of life did they have? I have since met many of their friends and some of their "children." All mentioned how wonderful they were, and how happy, but none knew anything about their private life. Why should they? The kind of beauty and love exemplified in this couple's life intrigues me and makes me feel that the glory of such unions is what we are trying to create. Because of the privacy inherent in such unions, we cannot provide a detailed picture for others. We will never know what suffering went on between these two because of their childlessness. Nor can we ever learn of their joy in living with the children of their neighborhood, nor about the flourishing of their bed. We may put the bits and pieces together from many such marriages, but we can get only a glimpse of the beauty of their lives together. Even though the evil stands out with dramatic intensity, the glory can be there too.

5 Problems
that arise in marriage

What has always made the state of hell on earth has been precisely that man has tried to make it his heaven. —F. Haelderlin
quoted in The Road to Serfdom *by F. A. Hayek*

Delayed development of female response

This chapter will be devoted to a consideration of problems arising in marriage. This is an artificial division since, as we have seen in the previous chapter, every problem that arises in marriage has roots reaching into the past, and branches that will spread into the future. However, for clarity's sake, it helps to make certain divisions and classifications to focus attention on a particular phase or aspect.

One problem that may arise after a couple marries is the delayed development of female response. This can be the source of some irritation and friction, because female sexual growth may often be delayed for years.

The husband may have expectations that are higher than are attainable. Reading overblown, lurid novels, which bear about as much relation to reality as fairy tales, and exposure to sex propaganda lead him to expect that his expertise will produce immediate and soul-shattering results. When this does not happen, he becomes frustrated and begins to blame her; and the whole process of growth is disrupted before it can become established. Sex then becomes an arena where the antagonists fight it out to various pathetic finishes—the divorce court, or the long war of attrition.

Even with patience he may find his technique is failing to produce much change, so his efforts gradually lose their enthusiasm. When she does show growth of response, he has already come to the conclusion that it really isn't worth all that effort. Biology continues pressing him, but an extra job and added expenses give him fatigue as an excuse. Frequency of coitus drops to once a week or once a month, and the emerging wife is puzzled and hurt that her sexual needs are not being met. She may attempt some aggressive measures and meet with failure. This is difficult for her to tolerate, and bitterness, invective and deep hostility develop.

The bride has learned about orgasm, too. She has been led to expect this as her right. She may even feel that she is entitled to every pleasure the man enjoys. The latent period of sexual response erodes her confidence in the male as a sexual partner. He responds to her attitude by losing some of his masculine ego. She tries to overcome this by becoming more aggressive and openly sexually attractive, but this inhibits him even more. The mechanism by which female aggression exerts improper and anti-sexual influence is shown by the classic example of the sterility patient who is asked to come into the office for the examination of sperm in the vagina after coitus. Quite a few have told me that they couldn't arrange for the test because their previously normal husband became impotent when they requested intercourse. When I questioned them on details, they admitted that they had announced at supper that it would be necessary to have coitus at seven o'clock so that they could be in my office at seven-thirty. They always seemed surprised when I told them that almost any man would be impotent under such a condition.

The clashes induced by these aggression conflicts make it difficult for me to understand how any couple's sex life can survive twin beds. The problems posed by the separation seem insurmountable. It is doubtful whether the most ingenious of couples sleeping in twin beds could manage the situation which follows. Let us assume Mr. Husband is saying goodnight to Mrs. Wife in bed. Her mood isn't very friendly, because he sat in his chair buried in the paper all night and never even told her what a nice supper she had cooked. He extends the good-night into a few questioning maneuvers, caressing her breasts and even bringing up the hem of her nightgown a little; but these are shaken off; or he gets the "roll away let me sleep" type of answer, so he moves to his side of a double bed. Just about the time he gets a little drowsy, he feels a toe wandering up his leg, or a hand reaching out for his. She has been thinking how patient he is and how one shouldn't hold a grudge—and he does kiss so nicely. How could these maneuvers be carried out in twin beds? The commitment is so definite and obvious, and the refusals so hard to withdraw from without losing face that it just seems to complicate an already complex affair.

Faced with the latent period and its problems, our couple must keep a number of things in mind. One is the fact that sex is just a part of marriage, not all of it. Sex is integrated with everything else that goes on; it is not in a compartment all by itself. Technique and books are not as important as attitudes and emotions. Our young man who is looking for a sexy wife should concentrate on living as a man before he worries too much about the bedroom.

Perhaps this can be illustrated by the story of two college chums, Fred and Joe, who met in the city twenty years after graduation. Not having seen each other since school, there was a great deal of laughter and talk about old times. Both had written occasionally and knew of each other's families. Fred noted that Joe was carrying candy and flowers, and he gave him a quizzical look. Joe caught the look, laughed and said, "I know what you're thinking, but you've got me wrong. I'm not chasing around; I'm still courting my wife."

It is difficult to say how a husband should try to cope with the latent phase in women's development, particularly when it is prolonged. Couples who bring this problem to a doctor should be allowed to talk about it freely. If a few discreet inquiries and a simple examination indicate that there are no major personality problems or physical defects, the solution is usually reassurance that they are normal, competent and capable, and that they must allow time for development.

A visit a few months later will generally show enough improvement to convince both that the situation is not hopeless. A part of each counseling session has to be concerned with debunking some of the exaggerated expectations that always exist. The doctor should also try to counter the massive miseducation which has taught the couple that human beings either are sexy or not sexy, instead of teaching them the truth that all human beings are sexual. Sexuality may start growing at age four, or two, or earlier; but it does not stop growing until forty or fifty.

When the wife lacks knowledge or her motivation is misdirected, the latent phase can continue to the point where she loses interest or even capacity to respond. We then speak of her as being frigid. As we noted before, frigid is not the right word. She isn't actually cold; she is unresponsive. If her husband approaches her without warning, uses little or no sexual foreplay or perhaps worse, goes through it mechanically, she may not respond, but her lack of response is not her fault. When the husband is inattentive all day, and then suddenly becomes attentive to satisfy his own desires, she resents his selfishness. If the moment he reaches his climax, he rolls over and goes to sleep, can we call her frigid because she fails to develop adequate response? These are the cases someone was thinking of when he said, "There is no such thing as a frigid woman; there are only clumsy husbands."

Love

Probably the most important factor in aiding the growth of sexuality for most marriages is the element of love with a capital "L." It is love that makes a young couple like each other's company night and day. It is love that helps them talk and laugh about a pretty miserable sexual misadventure while they lie in each other's arms in the dark afterward. It is love that makes the failures as good as the successes and takes the stuffiness out of the too technical or too intellectual approach. Don't we all recognize that sometimes the harder we try, the more we fail? Two people love and want each other for reasons beyond pure sex. Even if the sexual satisfaction never amounts to much, they can still build a good marriage. Millions have. Give these two a little help, and sex is no problem; it grows up as a part of their lives and flows over into the lives of their children.

Earlier we mentioned some of the difficulties the male

encounters, particularly on the honeymoon. Premature ejaculation was one of these. This is defined, in a very strict sense, as ejaculation before entrance. If this occurs after the honeymoon, it is pathological and requires treatment. A looser definition of premature ejaculation is ejaculation before the wife reaches her climax. This is extremely common. There is a male counterpart to the woman's growth in sexual response. This consists of his increasing ability in his approach to an act of coitus, plus his gradual acquisition of the ability to postpone his ejaculation and thereby prolong the intromission stage of intercourse. In the approach stage pauses for conversation and affectionate exchanges allow the male level of sexual stimulation to recede somewhat and yet do not seem to impair the woman's capacity for response. As long as the mood of love is sustained, such intermissions increase her personal involvement and reinforce her feeling of being desired, which is so important to her. In the intromission stage itself, pausing after entrance and continuing affectionate exchange bring her into more of a person-to-person relationship. Movement can be kept at a slow pace and in short thrusts to minimize the intensity of masculine sensation until such time as her response level is high enough. Clitoral stimulation can be used even during the intromission, particularly in the early years of the act.

Impotence in the male can be a temporary incident due to nervous tension or fatigue, or it can become a recurrent or chronic problem. Ninety or ninety-five percent of these cases are psychological in origin. The incidental occurrences are important only if they are overemphasized.

Changing role of women

In this situation modern women face some unusual problems.
Modern girls have been granted "freedom" in sexual matters;
but too often this freedom is not the relaxed sense of floating
with life that it should be. It is more a matter of having new
rules to live by. Now she must reach orgasm; she must neck
and pet. If she cannot enjoy this activity, she feels inadequate
or abused. If her stories do not match those of her friends and
the novels she reads, she feels crippled or defeated. More than
one college girl feels humiliated, because she remains a virgin.

The woman's orientation in sexuality is complicated by increasing social liberty. The large majority of girls working
outside the home before marriage and an increasing percentage
of wives working means that women come into fairly close
social contact with many men and cannot avoid making some
comparisons with the husband. The wife may have friends
who are having affairs before or between marriages, and she
may discuss sex and make sexual comparisons. These challenges
to the male may cause him to react by becoming more passive.
His sexual confidence and identity are threatened by two
sociological factors: the new economic and social position of
women, and a growing need for him to meet the expectations
of other people.

Women no longer depend on men for their livelihood; they
may even be competitors. The fact that there are many exceptions and that a particular man may have a so-called old-fashioned wife is of no importance, since he is affected by the total
image of women in the society. Instead of being a glorified
servant in the house, she is now co-partner, and even ruler

in many cases. Because his masculine image is jeopardized, and the expectations of his performance capacity are raised higher than before, our modern male is in a crisis. I suspect he will have more difficulties in the years ahead unless something drastic can be done. Unfortunate as it may be, marriage always has contained elements of rivalry. Now the previously weaker element has been given some new and better weapons. As a result, a new balance between the male and the female must be constructed.

All of this means that something extra must be added to marriage for today. There must be more preparation for it, more thought about going into it and with whom, and more instruction after the marriage ceremony. The only sociological mechanisms I can see which can help are the artificially contrived societies, such as Orwell's *1984*, or an increase in our understanding and use of love. At heart, I suppose I am an optimistic pessimist. I can look around me and see many things which I feel are very wrong and getting worse; and yet I have the feeling that this is just what mankind needs. We advance by facing and solving problems, and our increasing world population and urbanization make people the number one problem today. Personal relations and people's feelings about each other will occupy more and more of our scholars' time and effort. Out of this will come increasingly better ways of living together in peace.

Pregnancy

For at least eighty-five percent of marriages, pregnancy will enter the picture. Although this is the basic biological reason for, and the result of, sexual intercourse, it can also be viewed as a problem affecting the marriage. Just as it can be said that marriage will not help a personality problem, it can also be shown that children do not help a problem marriage.

I have had twenty-one years of extremely close association with pregnancy, having cared for and delivered almost 7,000 patients. The obstetrical problems are not too great a challenge. Most of them can be solved rather quickly. But the pregnant woman herself, her psychology, her feelings and her emotions are a constant challenge. I have the utmost respect for her courage and her dignity, but at the same time she often infuriates me with her unreliability, her changeableness and inconsistency.

There are three things about pregnancy the husband must concern himself with—and concern himself he must—because they are an integral part of his sexual role. Failure here can be as bad as, or worse than, failure with intercourse. The first is the desire to be pregnant, the second is the current pregnancy and the third is the wish either to avoid or to have a subsequent pregnancy. In our present society, with its increasing need for trained personnel, education has become more necessary and is of longer duration. This means that many couples have serious reasons for not wanting a child in the early years of marriage. It could be argued that such couples should postpone marriage, but this argument is fruitless from our point of view, since we are talking about people who are already committed. Other couples often wish to postpone the first pregnancy in order to allow more time for their personal relationship to become cemented.

There is no denying that pregnancy can come between a couple, so the validity of their argument has some force. Whatever the reason, and no matter how valid, the decision to delay pregnancy can create tension. This is again an illustration of the conflict between the intellectual and the emotional. This woman has excellent reasons for avoiding pregnancy, and she is fully convinced by her intelligence and common sense that this is a good decision; but as time goes on she becomes more irritable and hard to live with. She finds her job becoming more tiresome and boring, and life in general becomes a burden.

Her husband has noticed this, and one day, as they are coming home from work together, they stop and talk to a neighbor with a cute two-year-old boy. The husband plays with the child a little and then, later at supper, he finds his wife becoming sullen. Afterwards there is a quarrel.

As he thinks about it over the next few weeks he finds more evidence to show that, anytime she associates with children, spells of nervous irritability may follow. Fortunately, he is able to revise his plans. Without changing his objective, he sees how he can provide for a pregnancy and a child; and he suggests it to her. The minute he brings it up her eyes light up; but then the shutters drop, and she starts insisting it can't be done. He continues his presentation of the case, and she finally agrees that, if he really insists, maybe it would be a good idea to have a baby. If she doesn't manage to get pregnant in two or three months, she will be in some doctor's office for fertility study and will demand immediate results.

This same situation can arise in the period between pregnancies, and may happen even when the couple already has a large family. One of my patients had three children and had been taking anti-ovulation pills for over two years. She made an office visit which showed there would be a new pregnancy. When I asked her about the pills, thinking it might have been a case of drug failure, she admitted she had stopped taking them, because her husband had made her stop. At this point she began to cry and berate her husband for being a beast, a brute, and so on—all quite viciously. A month later she seemed more contented. When I remarked on her change of mind, she just looked at me, smiled and said, "If you ever tell my husband, I'll kill you, but I'm glad he made me stop."

Pregnancy itself is a trying time for any couple, but the first one is unusually trying for the husband. Local philosophers constantly make references to the unifying effects children have on a family. This is true in a long-term sense, but in a pregnancy itself the effects are divisive. I don't suppose any man, not even an obstetrician, can appreciate what it means to conceive and carry another human being inside of you. This overwhelming experience is so unique and personal that the male is on the fringe of its influence. The baby was, at one time, an important factor to him in the chain of the extended family relationship. But in today's personalized, nuclear family the infant does not assume its role in his life until its own personality begins to appear. He may consider it precious before this stage, but in the sense that it belongs to his beloved or, in some cases, because he has a role he expects the child to play for some personal reason.

It might be worth noting here that, while a wife has no doubt that a baby is her own, the husband can only be sure because of the trust he has in his wife. If she is having relations with more than one man, it is not possible to prove who the father is. It can be shown by blood tests that a certain male could not be the parent, but it cannot be proven exactly which one is the father. Perhaps this could be one of the greatest factors in encouraging restrictions on premarital sex relations and extramarital affairs. Research might show that increasing frequency of such practices erodes the male's image of himself as a father and creates a source of tension in this partnership, to which we assign the nurture of their child. If our system of monogamy is allowed to deteriorate, it would become necessary to devise a new system of child care.

The husband, therefore, must expect to feel somewhat neglected and abandoned. He will also feel battered psychologically, and this will be due to changes in the female hormone levels. These have already had some effect on his life, since they rise and fall during the menstrual cycle; and he may have experienced the sudden changes in mood and the emotional reversals which can accompany these shifts. The premenstrual phase in particular can be very annoying to both the wife and the husband. Many of what have been commonly called female characteristics are merely reactions to the changing levels of estrogens and progesterones in the bloodstream. One of the old Chinese characters in a Pearl Buck novel said, "A woman has the brain of a man, but it is bathed in the blood of a woman."

The point is that the husband must recognize that pregnancy is a time of stress and change, and that it imposes a rather unfair burden on the woman. After all, it would be much more equitable to have a system utilizing eggs and let him sit on them now and then instead of having her carry a twenty-pound tumor around inside her.

He must also recognize that she feels imposed upon and unattractive. Her old fear of desertion returns, but now there will be two left in the lurch, herself and the baby. She is convinced that she has lost all her power to hold him, and she needs all the reassurance she can get. It was pointed out earlier that pregnancy allows the male to develop his sexual role to its full capacity. Building on love with the patience that only love can bring, he should become her support, not her boss and not her errand boy. Maybe this is somewhat of a father image, but it is necessary.

One reason women are supposed to fall in love with their obstetricians is that he is a father image for them. The husband certainly should not be this. He should provide a calm base of support for her, a dependable sustenance to help her maintain some semblance of order and balance throughout this physiological crisis. He must walk a tightrope. If he is too sympathetic, there is no real support for her. If he is too helpful physically in running errands, he loses authority and his ability to support her. If he is too tired to help or feels she should keep busy, then he is "neglecting" her. There is one thing he cannot do wrong. He cannot give too much of himself; he cannot give too much reassurance; he cannot make her feel too needed; he cannot love her too much. This isn't the maudlin romanticism seen in movies, where he brings breakfast in bed and pats her pillow. No, this is the love of a man. This is the shoulder to cry on, the strong arms to enfold her and still her trembling. This is the shield who stands up to her mother when the latter starts interfering and meddling to the point that her visits produce tears.

During pregnancy, sexual intercourse itself is as variable as everything else. Some women will lose all desire for sexual relations, and others may become highly responsive, although they were indifferent before. Others will develop a marked aversion to the act of coitus, describing it as disgusting or revolting. The reasons for antagonism may be many, such as fear of harm to the fetus, the uselessness of the act from a procreative viewpoint; or the antagonism may be a form of punishment of the husband.

The cause probably cannot be determined, and it is not very important, since the condition is temporary. However, the husband does have to deal with the reluctance of his wife. He cannot retire into a peaceful abstinence, because she will then feel neglected, unattractive and abandoned. He must continue showing physical affection. Of course, this makes his frustration greater. By this time his appreciation of sexual intercourse has developed to the point where lack of interest on her part partially inhibits him, because without her participation it just isn't worth it. If she is properly motivated by love, she will manage some cooperation, particularly when his tension is high. It is detrimental for both to allow intercourse to go on when actual feelings of revulsion are present, since this can develop into a pattern of frigidity. If allowed to continue long enough, this might be difficult to reverse. Obstetricians vary in their instructions regarding coitus during pregnancy, but more doctors agree that it does not cause miscarriages and will probably do no harm in the last months of pregnancy, unless the bag of water is ruptured. Each patient, however, should follow the instructions of her own doctor. As the time for delivery approaches, the tension increases, because discomfort becomes more aggravating, particularly in multips, patients who have had previous pregnancies.

Structurally speaking, the human body is not fully adapted to walking on its hind feet and carrying a pregnancy in the upright position. This is really difficult when the abdominal muscles have lost their tone and capacity to support the full-term uterus. Since most women rarely do the exercises prescribed for them, each pregnancy becomes more difficult to carry. The more time she is required to spend on her feet, the more her legs, back and lower abdomen ache. Her ability lessens with each child, and her need to be up and about is increased.

In past years more help was available in the form of hired girls, relatives and friends. Often Aunt Samantha moved in for the last month or so and provided moral support as well as physical assistance. Older children could help, because they had few outside activities.

Today, hired help is almost unknown in our country, and relatives are far away and busy with their own problems. Her children, if old enough to help, are burdened with school activities or homework, and she feels guilty if she takes too much of their time. More and more she must depend on herself and her husband, thereby increasing the strain on their relationship. Psychologically, the fear of deformity or mental retardation places more stress on a system already burdened with physical and endocrine strain; so it is not surprising if she becomes short-tempered.

The following might be interesting as an illustration of how these fears wound the psyche. One Saturday night I received a panic-stricken call from a husband whose wife was due to deliver her fourth baby. He said his wife had suddenly collapsed on the floor and was lying there screaming and thrashing about. I could hear her in the background. Fortunately, he was in control of himself and could answer a few questions, so I was certain it was hysteria we were dealing with. I was on my way to the hospital and couldn't see her right away so I called a druggist for a strong sedative and gave the husband instructions on how to administer it.

He called me back in an hour to report that she was sleeping peacefully, so I asked him to bring her to the office the following Monday. She was calm and completely puzzled by what had happened. She revealed that the attack occurred when she was passing food to the children at supper and in particular, as she handed the four-year-old boy his plate. Discussion about worries, stories she might have heard, family problems, all were nonproductive. Finally, in desperation, I started asking her about Saturday, and we went through the day step by step. She told me about shopping at a local plaza. As she described walking from one store to another, she stopped and her eyes lit up as she exclaimed, "I know what it was!"

Then she went on to say that, as she walked along the mall in the plaza, she passed a woman from her neighborhood who had a mongoloid son. There is a fascinating simplicity about having the sight and memory of that woman register in the computer portion of the human mind. Then, as she is looking into the bright eyes of her own normal four-year-old, the circuits mesh; this terrible fear overwhelms her and causes that hysterical outburst that I could hear over the telephone.

Birth control

The third factor, which has an effect on the sexual life of a couple, is a developing fear of pregnancy when there are many children. This involves those couples who have religious beliefs which limit them to certain less effective methods of birth control, as well as large numbers of the very poor who find it difficult to plan for events that are nine months away when the problem of obtaining enough food for today has not been solved. So fear of pregnancy operates against them, too.

Any person who is constantly afraid of the consequence of a certain action is sure to be apprehensive about performing the action. Fear of pregnancy invades the whole area of affection. Couples are fearful of expressing even the simplest physical gesture lest natural desires may be set in motion and become difficult to stop. When affection does break through and leads to passionate embraces, stopping them often requires strong measures that leave hurt feelings.

The rhythm method

Intercourse may occur at the "wrong time" when a couple uses the rhythm method, despite their efforts to prevent it, and this means apprehension until the next period. Rhythm has been the butt of so many jokes and of so much oversimplified condemnation or promotion, that it seems hardly worthwhile to call for a calm appraisal. No one can deny that it imposes many difficulties for married couples. For some, the rhythm method may impede growth and advancement, but hundreds of thousands of couples practice it successfully. In many cases they have found that it improves their marriage. When periodic abstinence was chosen willingly, it offered the couple a chance to concentrate on love and sexuality, which then became more meaningful. Whether or not this happened depended on three things: the effectiveness of the method used to prevent pregnancy, the regularity of the woman's cycle and the attitude of the couple toward using the method. It often meant a liberation for some couples rather than a restriction, and the fostering of a dynamic, growing love in their lives.

When one backs away from the rhythm controversy and looks at it as a medical technique for birth control, a few things become evident. It is a very ineffective technique with a high degree of failure. Because of this it offers little security and brings no peace of mind to people who have reason to fear pregnancy for medical or economic reasons. Secondly, it imposes difficulties on the marital balance. Love is an emotion, a part of our feeling about things, and it is hard to regulate by the clock. If certain parts of the month are forbidden, this means the couple is forced to use another time; and the perversity of life is such that the week or ten days which is available is the time the two-year-old gets sick, so mother is in no mood. The only time available to a couple may be when they are fighting. There is no denying that rhythm can be highly destructive to the marriage relationship and can impose an intolerable burden on some couples. It is more than tragic to listen to a wife say she is coming to fear her beloved, and that she has to stifle every little affectionate action for fear of its consequences. The language of love is silenced. Please don't attempt to speak of spiritual love between husband and wife. This may be true for saints, but how many saints were married? In practice, I have lived and worked with couples who were using rhythm exclusively. During the period of toleration following Vatican II, when more and more Catholic couples utilized the progestin pills, or other birth control techniques, almost every patient commented on the marked improvement in marital harmony. For many of them it was the first time married love and sexuality became a factor in their lives, and they spoke of it with awe and reverence. As couples get older, coitus may become less frequent, but it is often more important and rewarding. The reaction may be more powerful, and under these circumstances rhythm can be impossible. Intercourse occurs with its natural variability, and, because they are busier, some of the most successful and most loving couples find that the burden becomes heavier as time goes on; and they recognize that rhythm is a major impediment to their union.

When pregnancy has occurred too frequently, it can become a permanent source of tension, because each act of intercourse acts as an irritant and a reminder of what has gone before, even though they have used some method of birth control, which makes possibility of pregnancy extremely remote.

Because reproduction and sex are so closely allied in the female view of things, any worry regarding the children and her role toward them will markedly affect the woman's sex life. This means that the husband's ability to fulfill his role as a father can be important to his success as her sexual partner. Our penchant for tagging certain words with great emotional connotations is nowhere more obvious than in the meaning we attach to the term "the head of the family." The phrase has been associated for so long with the tyranny of the old Victorian dictator-husband forcing his submissive wife into the position of a glorified servant that it is difficult to involve modern married couples in an intelligent discussion regarding the role of a husband.

Today we hear a great deal about married couples being partners, but I don't believe a wife is really happy with a partner. Marriage is not a partnership; it is a couple—two different people, one male and the other female, joined in a union for specific purposes. One is husband, and one is wife; one is father, and one is mother. Both are lovers. The head of the house is the man in the house. He is a tender, considerate anchor around which a home can be built. He provides the support for the wife and children, not always financial, but always psychological. He is dependable, because his biological structure is not upset by monthly variations in hormone levels. He is less emotionally labile and more capable of taking a detached, long-range view. There are infinite variations of this description, but it is not necessary that he fit himself into any classification but one. He must be the head of this family for this woman and these children. There is no time in marriage when the husband's role is as vital as it is during pregnancy.

Before leaving the subject of pregnancy, it will be necessary to comment on the role of the husband in the hospital at the time of delivery. The common picture of the foolish idiot seen in movies and cartoon strips is not worth mentioning. Most men are concerned, helpful and about as self-controlled as could be expected in a strange environment. His unusual behavior is due to fear of losing his wife through his own fault. After all, he started the whole thing. The fear would be lessened if more husbands would attend prenatal education classes to learn a little more about modern obstetrical techniques. Behavior ranging from extreme belligerence to running away and getting drunk is often due to their concern for their wives and their guilt feeling for being the real source of the trouble. Abandonment at time of labor and delivery can be a severe shock to the wife, and a source of sexual tension for a long time after the birth of the baby.

Many years ago I had a very lovely patient who was one generation removed from an Eastern European background. She was a truly beautiful woman, and her husband was a good, solid working-class man with an emphasis on the male. I had delivered her three times before and had never noticed anything unusual. But on the third day after this baby, I came into the room rather early one morning. I apparently caught her by surprise and found her crying quietly to herself. She was an extremely ladylike, self-possessed person so it shocked me; but I managed to get her talking, and she reluctantly told me the story. He husband was his own boss, and his work involved traveling, which he could schedule himself. With each baby there had been an extremely important customer who needed something urgently, so that he had never been around for any of the deliveries. He usually showed up about three or four days later. The last one had been just too much. She was all upset with vague anxieties about another woman.

Partly to reassure her, and partly because I believed it might be true, I mentioned that he might be staying away because he was afraid, and particularly afraid of losing her. She went on to tell me how wrong I was and how tough he was; a few drinks and look out, he might beat up everyone in the place. After some discussion, I got her to agree to a simple test. When he came to see her before taking her home, she was not to get upset or angry, but was to simply and quietly ask him if he was staying away because he was afraid.

The next day when I arrived, she was sitting up in bed with her eyes as big and as round as saucers. She was bursting with news, "Do you know what that big lug did when I asked him that question? He sat down in the chair and cried for five minutes."

It really wasn't hard to see. This "big lug," as she called him, had wrapped up everything that really meant anything to him in this lovely, beautiful woman who had chosen him. When he started courting her, he probably didn't think he had a chance, and he hasn't gotten over the surprise yet. If any fights did occur in taverns, it was probably because someone said something to or about her. She was truly the light of his life, and the fear that she might die or be injured by childbirth, as the result of his "dirty" impulses was just too much for him to bear. So he ran away from it all and suffered in a corner by himself.

Since this little scene, I have felt much closer to some of my frightened, obnoxious or belligerent husbands.

I have already discussed the problem of sterility. The wife's intense interest in getting pregnant can reach a point where she almost forgets her husband as a person and thinks of him only as an object to provide her with offspring. The husband may think of his wife only as a child-bearer, too. But this happens less frequently today than in former years. Years ago, husbands asked doctors to cure their wives of sterility. They ignored the possibility that they might be at fault and acted as though the wife was a prize heifer. Some men seem to have an extremely self-centered outlook. They flatly and force-fully reject any suggestion toward adoption, and entirely dis-regard the wife's emotional need for children to satisfy her mother instincts. The large majority of men recognize the paramount importance of this need in their wives and are fully cooperative; but too many are extremely resistant, and they cause a great deal of anxiety to the infertile woman. It is possible that the male confuses infertility with impotence. He may feel that getting his wife pregnant is a proof of his masculinity, but our explanations do not seem to change his mind very often. Needless to say, these marriages are operating under great tension, and sexual development is usually very poor.

Fatigue

Sometimes in attempting to analyze a problem or to explore a situation, the most obvious and simple facts are passed over, while attention is focused on the more intriguing portions of the question. In some cases of interrupted or impaired sexual development various Freudian aspects of the childhood are ex-plored, but the most common complaint of modern women is ignored. Numerous articles in medical journals are on the problem of feminine fatigue. Much effort has been expended in trying to find a solution for this ailment, but judging by the failure of various methods of treatment, an answer is not forth-coming. The relation between fatigue and sexual response in the female is obvious in that it creates inhibition toward the act in the first place; and it certainly interferes with the ability to respond, since this is a physical effort in which a good deal of energy is often expended. Psychiatrically-oriented writers often claim that fatigue is an excuse to mask the discomfort of frigidity. This can be true in a small number of cases, but there would be no reason for all these women to crowd docors' offices and go through various blood tests, etc., to try to alleviate such fatigue. Other writers claim that fatigue is a symbol of boredom and indicates the woman's lack of fulfillment in her role as mother and housewife. Again, there may be an element of truth.

I will leave a complete analysis of the problem to others; but in our context it is useful to realize the detrimental effects it has on sexual growth and to consider two possible causes. The first of these two is lack of exercise. Modern Americans travel by wheels more and more, and we exercise less and less. Our only way to break this cycle is for each person to establish a daily program of lifetime exercise. The dividends for such a program are many, among which are the reduction of coronary heart attacks among our younger men, and a general sense of well-being in both sexes. Most athletic activities are not maintaned regularly enough to be of much value. A persistent, sensible program is the only answer. This may help reduce fatigue by building up reserve power and avoid having so many persons working near the limit of their ability. If you want to run a mile, you practice running five miles; then the mile seems, and is, much easier. Improvement of general physical conditioning and ability enables a person to develop the physical stamina needed for a more active sex life and allows for some escape from routine and boredom. There is no harm in having a variety in marriage, and why bother looking outside for variety if it can be found at home?

The second element that creates excessive fatigue for women is the job of maintaining a home and rearing children. In the first place, what about hours? How many days a week is the employee expected to work? How about time off for vacations? What about the possibility of promotion in the sense of a change of pace, the chance to look forward to something different? A work day lasting from seven in the morning to ten at night is certainly not unusual, and a seven-day week is standard. Time off is for shopping trips, an afternoon out with the girls or a night on the town now and then. When they do get time off, the help is often inadequate, and there is a good deal of guilt about leaving the children. Certainly some women run away from this responsibility. They may even rationalize their guilt by talk of community responsibility, but using such excuses, even when they are legitimate excuses, is a difficult and nerve-racking process.

As for vacations, anything involving the children is not a vacation; it is a trip, and it is of little value for the mother, even when she is not burdened with cooking and housework. As for promotions or change, there aren't any for mothers. When she graduates from Cub Scouts, there are the Boy Scouts. When her children are old enough to sleep through the night, they start going out on dates, and the mother is either sitting up waiting, or sleeping a twisted sleep that only a mother knows when her young are out on the highways in a modern high-speed automobile. These are the facts of life, and I am sorry I have no nice solutions; but I think that, if the problem were brought into the open, more couples would find ways to arrange for rest breaks for the mother. Some couples find part-time help from high school girls in the neighborhood. Some women have an exchange system where one takes the other's children for the afternoon.

Two couples I know have an exchange weekend plan. Every three months one couple takes all the children and converts the house into a barracks. Games are organized and meals are simple. Equipment is moved by rented trailer, and they tell me it is run like an army maneuver. The children never see each other except for these weekends, so the element of newness inhibits the furor for at least a while. The other couple spend the weekend in a local motel, and three months later the whole precedure is reversed.

Some have solved the vacations by camping, or camper trips, where father and the boys are in complete charge of all cooking, packing, etc.

I think more married couples should be spending weekends in motels. Let's get the married couples in so there won't be room for the others. Cost is important; but some families are spending far more on doctor, or even hospital bills, to take care of a nervous mother than it would cost to spend many weekends in motels.

People who comment on extramarital sexual affairs as a natural part of life, because sex is bound to become boring under the restrictions of monogamous marriage, are only indicating the superficiality of their knowledge and the poverty of their humanity. Sexual activity can become boring for some people, but so can flying an airplane. Sexuality is a part of being a person, and truly human persons are too complicated to become boring. People never become boring unless one stops looking at them and listening to them; or if one was only using them in the first place. Looked upon as a purely physical activity, sex might die, since there is a limit inherent in this aspect of its nature. Experimentation, with all conceivable variations extending even into the zone of perversions, could eventually exhaust the element of newness in the object. Then there would be nothing further to seek except to attempt a new beginning with another partner. With each recurrence of this maneuver the element of "something new" would last for shorter and shorter periods. Sexuality cannot fall into this state of ennui, because too much of the person is invested, and the only road to failure lies in the vacuity of the persons involved. Those limited in their humanity or their ability to express humanity, either by self-directed or externally imposed restraints, cannot go far in any direction.

Extramarital affairs

Something that every husband should engrave deeply into his consciousness is the devastating effect extramarital affairs have on a wife. You have to sit with one of these patients as she slowly and reluctantly, and with pain and humiliation, tells her story. There is no doubt that the male is equally devastated by such aberrant behavior, and his hurt pride can cause violent reactions extending to the classic crime of passion; but the woman's need for love, her need to be needed and her evaluation of her importance place her personality structure in jeopardy. When children are present, the fear of desertion is compounded, since it means a threat to the security of her home and her children. Perhaps she reacts so strongly, because she would not be likely to cheat unless she no longer loved her husband. Normal women do not have sexual relations with men they do not love. This may be a cultural attitude rather than a basic element in her psychology; but it is there, nevertheless. So-called modern women may bring a different and more tolerant attitude into marriage, but I do not see many of these avant-garde wives in my office; and I doubt that there are many in our society, despite the opinions of some writers and publications.

Incidents of cheating which occur during the wife's pregnancy are doubly soul-shattering, since her confidence in her attractiveness and in her ability to hold her husband are already out of balance. No amount of explanation can convince a woman that her husband's peccadillos are entirely different from any similar activity on her part, and she cannot understand that his "affair" could be due to the urge of the moment and exist even in face of deep and honest love for her. Because she gives herself only in love, she assumes this is true for him; and she sees the affair as a total disaster to her marriage. Such shocks can be overcome with patience and understanding, but the scars remain and would certainly focus on the act of intercourse as the center of the problem. Impaired development, or even regression of a previously well-developed reaction on the part of the wife, would not be totally unexpected.

I am sure that I will be vilified by many for saying this, but I still believe that the double standard exists. I am not promoting it, and I do not see it as an excuse for license on the part of the male; but I recognize it as a fact of life for many people. The best explanation I can offer is as follows: "It is all right if I have intercourse with *your* sister, but it certainly is not all right for you to have intercourse with *my* sister."

There is also a difference between the reasons why the wife cheats and the reasons why the husband cheats. There is no excuse for either one. But an explanation of the differing psychology of men and women may give some understanding of the reasons why men and women cheat each other. Such an explanation may possibly repair some of the damage.

When a wife cheats, it may be because of an emotional disorder, alcoholism, a bad marriage, or because she is in love with another man. Today, an added reason might be that she has acquired a masculine outlook on things and can tolerate sex as an incident. If the latter is true, it opens to serious discussion the exact status of her femininity. If she is going to cheat, all the children in the marriage will become suspect to her husband. Although she is always biologically certain that it is her baby, he can only assume the baby is his on the basis of trust.

Males may cheat for any of the same reasons, but more frequently their cheating is only a casual incident that means nothing. It may be a sex act that more resembles an act of masturbation than it does an act of intercourse, a mark of immature development of sexuality and a lack of understanding as to its true nature. I have little use for cheating husbands, because the damage they render to the marriage can be incalculable; but each case must be understood for its own causes. Oversimplified interpretations can be dangerous and can prevent any repair of the ruptured marriage union. The cheating husband who is found out, and whose wife denies him intercourse for months afterwards, forcing him to court and win her over again, has no complaint. He is lucky to have an understanding wife.

The things some women do in such cases is fascinating. Many years ago one of my patients, with four children and still young at twenty-four, found her husband was having an affair with a twenty-two-year-old girl in her neighborhood. He often called on his friend in the late afternoon. One day she dressed all the youngsters in their finset, and, with their faces all shiny and hair all combed and braided, she paid a call on the girl about an hour before her husband was due to arrive. By the time he got there, the two women were good friends, and they politely took turns belting him with frying pans. The marriage was salvaged, and my patient was matron of honor when the girl married a few years later. I can only hope that the husband came to realize that he had quite a woman for a wife, and that he finally learned how to handle her with proper care and love.

Absentee husbands

A peculiar situation that exists in many marriages now is a source of tension. Although it does not have a direct effect on sexual intercourse, it does have a great deal of influence on the outcome of its growth and development. This is the problem of absentee husbands—policemen, firemen, corporation executives, doctors, salesmen and others whose jobs require absences from home for varying periods. This strikes at the woman's Achilles' heel of loneliness and abandonment. When children are in the picture, it means she is carrying the responsibility of rearing them to a greater extent than she should. Often nothing can be done about such situations, although the employers involved should pay more attention to the strain they are imposing upon their men. They should also institute some studies on the matter and organize some efforts to help.

If the husband recognizes that his job imposes a burden on his wife by increasing her sense of loss and feeling of loneliness and by making her feel that she has all the responsibility for the children, he can make certain countermoves to compensate for the difficulty. Frequent phone contacts during absences, particularly in the evening, and listening to all the talk about the children will help.

Men too often assume that a rapid fire of words from the wife is just chatter, but sometimes it has more meaning than appears at first glance. Her recital of all the details of the children's activities during the day is her way of passing some of the responsibility to him. His listening without objection is approval of what she has done. It allows her to pass part of the responsibility over to him, and to rid herself of the oppressed feeling of having everything hinge on her. Allowing such tension to continue building up, not knowing where it comes from or how to cope with it, can prove extremely destructive to any relationship, and particularly to one as delicate and finely balanced as the sexual union between man and wife.

Related to the previous outgrowth of the economic side of marriage is the tension in marriage generated by the practice of large corporations of moving their executive personnel about the country. This practice is far more disturbing to the wife and children than it is to the husband, because their roots are in their home and neighborhood. Frequent moving dislodges children from the neighborhood and friends with whom they have been trying to establish firm relationships. It involves more strain on the children, because their task of familiarization in a new place is much greater. We are only learning to appreciate the child as a small human being who differs especially in the proportion of newness he encounters every day. The wife's closer association with and increased awareness of the child's feelings makes her more sensitive to this and causes a great deal of inner disturbance and conflict. The husband's job may be interesting to him and economically rewarding, so she hesitates to trouble him. Yet the children have more problems with every move, until the situation may finally explode. In many cases the tension erodes the union between two people; and the marriage slowly distintegrates with sexual failure, extramarital affairs or just plain chronic despair. I doubt if corporations realize how much this can cost them in impaired efficiency among executives or supervisory personnel.

One fascinating cause of such moves can be the executive whose own marriage has deteriorated completely, so he is completely cold to any complaints about such moves. He may actually be getting even by transferring others more or less needlessly. This is one portion of a corporation's social responsibility that I have never seen discussed. The armed forces have the same problem; and they are faced with mass resignations, many of which are not really based on the high pay available on the outside, but on the destructive effect of frequent moving on the wife, children, and husband-wife relationship.

6 Sexual growth and emotional maturity

> *The mature man . . . learns to live with imperfections—in himself, in others, and in society—without making a standard of imperfection.*
> —*John J. Hallowell*, The Moral Foundations of
> Democracy

The real objective of human medical practice is prevention. Cures are sought and desired, but the acme of perfection is the elimination of disease wherever possible. Medicine concerns itself with behavior when this becomes destructive or disturbing, and particularly so when emotional disorders carry physical changes or symptoms, or markedly affect organic diseases. Enough is known today of psychiatry to describe in some detail how we grow and develop to maturity, and so we are able to note what can assist such growth and what can impede it. Everyone has heard misbehavior referred to as childish. We speak of childish quarrels in marriage, of the childishness of jealousy, and so on. Maturity is the goal we all seek, and it is universally agreed that with mature behavior many problems would be solved quickly and easily. If we develop an adult outlook, our problems of living together, raising children and improving our world will practically solve themselves.

Maturity is the goal

It is obvious that the human path of development is from the totally parasitic fetus to the independent and more or less self-sufficient parent capable of being responsible for spouse and children. In another sense, mature biological development consists of capacity to live free of the parental organism and to take on the responsibility for offspring. Starting from the parasitic role of the fetus, the human being moves on through sucking, crawling, walking, to learning social amenities such as the use of bathroom, crossing streets, etc. Going off to school is a very big move, and the child gradually progresses by developing more ability, more capicity and more knowledge. When adolescence appears, growth is almost completed; and the energy that is no longer needed for growth can be directed outward and expended in mating, in sexual productivity and in taking on the responsibility of caring for others.

The long years of our childhood tend to leave us with a taste for the pleasures of childhood. We look back on the days of freedom from responsibility and long for the dependence on parents. Maybe because we were children so long, we never really get over it. The central conflict for adolescents is the growth toward freedom and independence and the fear of becoming responsible for the care of others. When trouble arises, there is regression—the age-old flight back to childhood, to mother's arms. Unfortunately, many parents try to hold back the children and try to remain protective even when their children are married. These married children are almost encouraged to regress at the first sign of difficulty. As adults we may continue to want dependence, perhaps because we missed it as children, or because we had too much of it. When this is so, our normal development is impaired, as is our capacity to live in emotional independence and self-reliance.

Some adults are never able to outgrow this dependence. They will continue throughout their adult years to live and react emotionally as children. Being incapable of coming to terms with responsibility, they regress into the inconsistent, erratic and often bewildering behavior of children. Those who do this consistently are in extreme difficulty most of the time and do not succeed in adult emotional living.

I have seen a patient whose husband could not cope with the responsibilities and left the marriage to return to his mother; but he continued to date his "wife" and insist that he really loved her. She worked and supported her two children for some years until she met a really mature man who convinced her that divorce and remarriage was her only chance. She got a divorce and remarried despite the fact that her church forbade it.

Other husbands are more capable and operate well until some difficulty arises to cause regression. Then they retreat into some infantile form of behavior. Others have a strong desire to retreat, but they suppress it by strength of will, only to have the defenses generate inner tension, which causes a variety of symptoms. A fully mature individual is independent and maintains his function even in the face of great frustration.

In the human organism, progress from parasitism on the mother to relative independence increases capacity for responsibility and productivity and decreases receptive needs. Part of the adult's sense of responsibility lies in his ability to consider the consequences of his actions. Maturity consists of conditioning and training for socialization and domestication.

This is not, or should not be, enslavement. It is a development of conscience, particularly social conscience. It is a part of the inner tendency toward cooperation, not a negative restraining force, but an innate tendency of growth toward independence, responsibility and cooperation. Because of too little or too lax development, we see infantile, impulse-ridden adults. Because of too much training and too harsh discipline, we see anxious, inhibited individuals overburdened with pathological consciences. Conscience makes us look for danger in what we do or what we say, but it should allow us the freedom to make mistakes and the intelligence to recognize them.

We are not always capable of realizing the danger inherent in what we do or say, but we can at least look for trouble, take warnings seriously and avoid making too many mistakes. I once heard it said that the Lord may forgive ignorance, but he can't forgive stupidity. A driver who, on a strange road, comes upon a railroad crossing around a curve and doesn't see the train coming is ignorant. The one who knows the crossing is there, but who assumes that, because the lights are not flashing, there is no train coming and doesn't bother to look for a train is stupid. Someone who makes a mistake once or twice may be ignorant, but a person who makes the same mistake over and over again is either stupid or psychiatrically disturbed.

As children we develop our ability to control emotions such as anger, or sexuality along with our movement toward maturity largely through the incentive of being loved. When unloved, or deprived of a full degree of it, we care little about controlling ourselves; and socialization and smooth, progressive emotional growth is disturbed. Perhaps this explains so much of the behavior of our youth with their cry for freedom that overrides the needs of others and results in so much antagonizing behavior. The base of our emotional life is in the ability to love and be loved, to give and to receive, to work, play and rest.

Another characteristic of maturity is relative freedom from feelings of inferiority. The competition for prestige between husband and wife is often based on this. They struggle to demonstrate strength against the other in a multitude of almost incomprenhensible, childish ways. A mature male or female derives satisfaction from the productive use of his powers which is basically kind, cooperative and responsible. The male's sexuality is a means of reaching out to his wife, of telling her something he cannot put into words, of bringing her closer to him. When it does not accomplish this, it is useless. When she desires a child, he wants to give her one. If a child frightens or overburdens her, he doesn't want any at this time. The wife's sexuality is her way of being attractive, of bringing him into her where she holds him and knows him, of helping him retreat temporarily from the troubles and turmoil outside. It is her way of creating a new part of him—the only immortality every human being is really sure of.

Modern psychoanalytic studies are beginning to trace the development of the sexual appetite through infantile stages to what is called the genital level, with its mature capacity for "object interest," and interest in people, with the capacity for love and productivity, both social and sexual. The latter is an important part of the total emotional development. Sexuality has a double relationship to emotional growth. It is a powerful force in itself, and it is an expression of the individual's particular makeup and degree of development, along with being a channel for the drainage of all kinds of feelings and impulses. It leads the young from dependence on the parents to being parents themselves. Because it moves people toward the responsibility of loving, supporting and caring for a family, it should be a powerful push toward maturity. When sexuality does not evolve properly, the *whole process of emotional growth can be influenced.*

It is true that excessive repression in the past impaired the freedom and ease of functioning as an adult and interfered with mating, or impaired sexual growth and satisfaction. But excessive freedom in childhood and youth may prevent the integration of sexual growth with the rest of development, and it may block the channeling of this growth into the capacity for learning to love and raise a family or to live in a marriage. Sexuality remains childish in nature. It continues as a matter of play and personal pleasure, but never as a part of a real adult life.

The *"playboy"* philosophy

As noted above, the whole process of emotional growth can be influenced. This is basically what is wrong with what has been called the "playboy" philosophy. This concept brings out into very sharp focus the subtly vicious "game" aspect of sexuality. The poor man caught in this web becomes frozen in his development at a child level, and its influence impedes any real growth of sexuality. You cannot really know what a beautiful breast is until you have seen a young mother nursing. You cannot realize the beauty of women unless you see them in pregnancy, and there is no real sexuality except in a marriage, or a marriage-like situation.

The incidence of frigidity among "bunnies" and playgirls would be astonishingly high, although admittedly hard to detect. The men caught up in this movement are ruining our young girls in ways far more damaging than the few illegitimate pregnancies that may occur. Already I have noted antagonism in my younger patients based on "pawing" and "all he wants from me is . . .", etc. She looks for love, and he offers her an affair. He bases his approach on his "terrible" frustration and on how "natural" his feelings are. The most unnatural thing in the world is sexual intercourse separated from procreation.

Perhaps all this is culturally imposed, but, if you want to offer a woman sexual relations based on the mores of a South Sea island tribe, you had better provide her with their methods of raising and caring for children and be prepared for a marked shift in her personality and outlook. Don't expect any deep male-female relationship or union, and forget the word "love." Our whole society and culture would have to be adapted to fit. This is a fantastically complex, interlocking structure, and meddling with it is more disastrous than some amateur electrician trying to repair a computer circuit.

In a way, modern youth has been caught in a bind. An injustice was done to them when the old strict rules fell apart, and a certain amount of tolerance was brought to bear. Out of compassion, many of the older generation began to say that premarital intercourse was not the horrible tragedy it had been claimed to be. With the development of more effective means of birth control, the fear of illegitimate pregnancy was *supposedly* reduced, but it was never meant to be a question of promoting such activity. This promotion was taken up by a few fools here and there, along with a large number of the young men, for various and immediate reasons. These voices were magnified in the communications media because of their news value. Foolishness, like crime is always publicized.

The effects of permissive attitudes are spreading like wildfire.

I am a Chardinian optimist; and although I am fully convinced that a hundred thousand years from now intelligent life in the universe will have progressed in a remarkable manner, I am rather pessimistic about the progress of the human race in the next hundred years. I am afraid this present trend will have to run its course. More and more of these playboys will attempt to marry their bunnies, and bring up children. The divorce rate will climb, and there will be greater problems among children and increasing violence to the human psyche.

To attempt to warn a modern young person of the danger involved in letting the bars down is a difficult and almost overwhelming task. Long-term dangers are always hard to see, mental hazards will forever be vague, and the subtle aspects of human nature are just plain difficult to demonstrate and explain. It was very easy to say, "Look out, you might get pregnant."

For the girl in particular, the consequences were easily visualized and felt. To point out today that starting intercourse before marriage is an irrevocable move, which will change the whole course of sexual growth and influence the entire process of emotional development, is not as simple and dramatic as the older, "Don't do this, or else. . . ."

Young couples near them in age who made this move a year or so before them are markedly in favor of premarital intercourse and highly recommend it. Look at them. They are having "a ball." Those ten years older, married and with children, who are living lives torn apart with mental anguish, consuming tranquilizers by the ton, are not being asked, and they are probably in too much pain to talk about it. The advocate of the take-it-easy approach is forced to plead, to pray and to suffer as he watches so many sheep gambol into what may be worse than a slaughterhouse. I can think of no other words except, It's an awful mess. I have listened to them —hours at a time.

I am not retreating into the old game of scare the hell out of them. If my remembered secondhand misery makes me overeloquent, please forgive me. As we live today, failure will happen, and one fall is not a disaster. A mature human being makes mistakes and continues to do so, but he can pick himself up and still maintain a sense of direction. Anyone knows that, if you are climbing a mountain and fall a short way, you don't keep rolling downhill. You fight to hang on; and then, bruised as you are, you keep staggering towards the top and level ground. This flexibility and adaptability is all part of another characteristic of a mature adult. There is a world of difference between tolerance and approval. We can be tolerant of a couple who succumb to natural forces; and yet we can retain our disapproval of what they are doing. Our disapproval is based on fear of the harm they may be doing to themselves and to their future children, if and when the union fails to be properly established, or is distorted by their indiscriminate action.

Such disapproval should never be based on a good person versus a bad person viewpoint, but on a concept of doing something potentially harmful to themselves and others. Maturity means responsibility, and responsibility requires a view toward the future and beyond the immediate. An interesting sidelight on maturity is that it not only represents these and other attitudes and functions we have discussed; but it also bestows on us the ability to enjoy them fully.

Naturally, none or at least very few of us, ever really achieve such levels of maturity. These are the ideals. No one can make himself mature by willing it; but, by remaining aware of what it really is, he can keep moving in the right direction. We all recognize that in every man there remains some of the boy. This gives him humor and the ability to play. We also should realize that some reach maturity at sixteen, and many at fifty aren't there yet. One of the tragic things an obstetrician sees almost every day is the lovely young child-bride who becomes a woman during her pregnancy and delivery, and her fine young husband who is being left behind and estranged from her by this widening gap in emotional years.

In any consideration of maturity, sexuality must occupy a prominent place. It is important in the first place, because of its biological force and the impetus it brings to the growth process; and, secondly, because it is a pathway for the expression of all kinds of emotional impulses and tensions, and because it has such a pervasive influence on personality growth and development.

As noted before, a central fact in this biological force is its connection with reproduction. The male, in particular, tends to attempt to ignore this, as is brought our vividly in the "playboy" philosophy. The essential and tragic error of male-centered sexuality is that it loses sight of the central fact that sex has something to do with reproduction. Because nature is so bountiful and provides so many more sperm and egg cells than could ever be utilized, plus a generous bonus of pleasure, it is rather obvious that when this great tide of sex is restricted it spreads out in many forms that often seem remote from reproduction. But the essential stuff of sex is still sperms and eggs; and the central purpose is reproduction, with all the consequences, such as responsibility for the partner and the family. This is adult sexuality. Anything else is childish, and any side-tracking means impairment of normal sexual development. This is why the male partner in an infertile marriage has to deal, not only with a frustrated wife, but also with the big problem of helping her grow into a responsive bed partner.

The reason for discussion of emotional maturity is that persistent immaturity, or childish emotional patterns, are destructive in marriage. Statements such as, "I wish he would grow up," are common. Long discussions in the older popular writings on marriage revolved around the question of the man's right to go out with the "boys." The word is a dead giveaway. Certainly a man needs the company of men now and then, but not the company of "boys." A mature person has the capacity to play and is adaptable enough to want exposure to all facets of life. Fishing trips, sailing, athletics, etc., with other men are a change of pace. They develop and expand various aspects of a person's mind or interests; but he doesn't need them to escape from his family. In fact, he suffers when he is absent too long. He becomes lost when separated from home, wife and children. He loves men, but not in the way he loves his wife and children. There is pleasure and fun in games or bull sessions, but there is joy in the home. His wife does not feel abandoned when he goes out with men for a man's reasons, but she is lost when he retreats into childhod and goes out with the boys.

A mature woman doesn't hold onto her husband in panic and resent every moment of separation. She feels confident in herself as a woman and in her love with its ability to draw her husband close to her. Business separations and time in men's company is no threat to her position. The child is the one who fears abandonment and cries, "Daddy, don't leave me." The adult child can smother the man with a travesty of love, which gradually pushes him farther away, until the union is broken or irreparably damaged. This is the woman who can become a hypochondriac by constantly playing up her weakness, until she actually impairs her health and functions at a lower and lower level of efficiency.

Immaturity leads to erratic and irresponsible behavior. This behavior initiates a self-perpetuating and destructive relationship, which becomes increasingly difficult. Unless some drastic event brings things to a head, or the couple become aware of the direction they are taking and do something about it, their relationship will deteriorate. The majority of money conflicts have their basis in immaturity. The wife who expects to move into a house like her mother's and wants all her furniture and equipment as soon as the time payments will allow is certainly acting like the child who grabs every toy she finds and says, "Mine, mine." The wife who will not sacrifice her immediate desires for the future is certainly living in a child's world of everything-for-now with no thought for the future. The woman who expects her husband to continue taking her out on "dates," despite the strain on their budget, is not capable of planning for the future and is violating one of the central norms of maturity.

The impulse-ridden personality is part of this immaturity complex and is very difficult to get along with in marriage. The husband stops in a bar on the way home from work and meets some friends; so he stays there and perhaps even goes out with them for supper, despite the fact that his wife is waiting supper at home for him. He forgets that she may be frantic with thoughts of his lying injured in a hospital or even dead in a morgue. He comes home and actually resents the fact that she is upset. After all, he put up with that for years with his parents. Now she is acting the same way. She wants to know where he was and what he was doing.

The anger and frustrated irritations which meet her honest, well-meant questioning seem completely unreasonable to a mature woman. They can be understood only when and if she can comprehend all the facts that go into causing the outburst. When we can achieve the ability to look at ourselves a little, it is always helpful to know both our weaknesses and our strengths. By doing this we can learn to grow a little more in our own quest for maturity. However, the most understanding and capable wife imaginable can come up against a situation whose background is so deeply entrenched that her love and understanding cannot produce any change in his understanding and behavior. When this happens there is no choice but to seek professional help. Knowing when the point of futility is reached is difficult and impossible to describe; but the persons involved usually come to realize it, because the feeling that something must be done gets stronger with each recurrent crisis. They must realize that something *can* be done and that professional help, although sometimes difficult to find, is available.

Maturity in relation to the job

Many couples quarrel over the husband's job. In some cases an aggressive wife keeps urging a passive husband to assert himself more, to change jobs, or to insist on a raise. This might be termed a conflict in styles of living, and for some it may be a good thing. No one should place himself on a pedestal as a sensible, mature, all-knowing arbiter of humanity. All of us have what might be called defects which yet contribute to our lives and those around us. Some passive men are helped by this prodding and become highly successful; but if some other man did exactly as his wife wished, the boss would fire him, and he might sink into depression and repeated failures. Since his own style of living made him hesitate about asking for a raise, it might take a year or more of pushing on the part of the wife to get him to do it. By that time the boss may be receptive to the idea of the raise. He may even feel that it shows the man really has the get-up-and-go to deserve a promotion, which he had not previously considered him for. In many cases the job problems may be the remnants of childhood conflicts, which were never resolved. He is rebelling against authority, but because he has no skills or training to back up his requests, he is fired. Forced by family responsibility to get work as quickly as possible, he must take an even worse job. The same problem continues to recur, and the family tension rises until the marriage is destroyed.

Economic crises are precipitated when a husband's anger bursts out at work for little or no reason. Finally, he is "let go" to maintain peace in the office or plant. Such anger is often recognized and described as childish by those who see or feel it. They do not realize that his outbreaks are based on the frustrations of this thirty-five-year-old man's own childhood.

There are some interesting studies showing the effect certain occupations have on abnormal behavior. Men with extremely bad records for job stability, or with police records for drinking, fighting or petty crime, go on for years like this until they land in a certain line of work. Suddenly a complete change takes place. They become steady workers with no police record, and sometimes they are very successful. Not all can find jobs to fit their psychological needs, so that the woman married to one of these vocational misfits is in for a very rough time, unless she can help him work out his problem or obtain help in doing so.

A very difficult situation comes up when a man wants to quit his job and go into business for himself. In almost every man there is some boy, and since almost every woman wants someone to mother, this works out fine; but when a man dreams and plans for the future ten or twenty years hence, his wife may think it is all pretty foolish. One of my patients talked about this problem. She complained that her husband wanted to quit his job and open a TV repair shop.

In 1947 the idea of earning a living repairing TV's seemed ridiculous, because only a few very rich people owned TV's then.

"How will we pay the rent?" she demanded. "He says he likes to work with people and that his buddy, who is an expert radar repairman, will work with him. But what difference will that make? I don't know even one person who has a TV set. If he quits his job, he won't get a paycheck. How foolish can a man be?"

I let her talk, and then I explained that her husband had always been reliable and steady. He had worked hard setting up the business, and he had a good partner. Besides that, every man had to do what he thought was right, or he wouldn't be a man. I don't know if my talk helped, or how he won out; but he did. Now, twenty years later, he has one of the largest TV centers in the area. The wife has a right to be really concerned when these ventures come one after the other, always end in failure, and are never planned ahead of time. The childishness stands out in the hours and hours of talk about a new project, but no investigation, no visits to people who know something about a business and no serious planning. The immaturity is sometimes obvious in the prospective partner who is as ignorant and as ill-prepared for the venture as he is. A word of warning. No wife should get too upset about talk. A man must dream, and some of this is dreaming and dream talk. Some men go all through their lives talking about the business they are going to start, the trip up the Amazon, or how they are going to retire to the South Seas or Florida. If someone handed them the money to do it, their heart would be broken—like the dream.

Jealousy

Jealousy is one of the facets of human nature which can be a vice or a virtue depending on how, when, and to what extent its force is allowed to exert itself. Defined as being watchful or solicitous, it is a sensible virtue and recognized as such by most couples. If a husband finds that his wife's eyes flash a little; and she starts a conversational migration from across the room toward him when a pretty girl stops to talk to him at a party, he should, and probably will, be flattered by her alertness and attention. The wife would probably react in the same manner when she found that whenever a nice young man paid attention to her, the husband appeared at her side quietly, and with an appropriate delay, from out of nowhere.

However, if the husband finds his wife barging in on the polite conversation he is having with the boss's spouse or daughter, she becomes a chattering, conversational bulldozer who tears up the social landscape, instead of the bright social asset he expects. The opposite situation occurs when her quiet talk with the new salesman in the company is interrupted by a charging linebacker bent on "red dogging" the quarterback —his wife—right out of the play. Jealously based on insecurity and feelings of inadequacy is often uncontrollable, and it is truly devastating in a marriage. It causes storms, the effects of which linger for weeks afterward, and, worst of all, the storms come again and again. This childish reaction is fixed, and it dominates behavior so thoroughly that the stubborn repetition occurs despite all the well-meant and most sincere promises never to do it again.

One of the tragic twists in this particular problem is that jealousy is often appealing before marriage. To the girl about to be married, a jealous fiance is attentive, is thinking of her and fulfills her need to be wanted. To the boy whose mind at this time is totally involved with her, jealousy is true possession. The bridegroom has eyes only for the bride, and no one expects him to be much more than polite to his boss's wife. A few months or a year later, life reaches a balance. Since a child is coming, he must think of the economic and social side of marriage; so he will begin to resent interference from her. Note that all discussion here refers to unfounded jealousy. Any husband who has a record of infidelity in marriage must expect his wife to be more sensitive to threats and more intolerant of any contacts with potential rivals, including the boss's wife.

This is one of the side effects of the playboy mentality. How is it possible to expect a "bunny," who knows her husband's premarriage philosophy of having fun, to be a secure, tolerant and relaxed wife? And, if the bunny was a real playgirl before marriage, why shouldn't her husband move in immediately every time he sees her with a man? Those contemplating marriage should be cautious about unreasonable jealousy. If jealousy bothers a person before marriage, it will be worse in marriage. This could be said about any problem in behavior. The person whose drinking is troublesome in dating, the careless spender, or the flighty girl who constantly leaves you in the lurch will not improve. Marriage does not cure problems. It usually makes them worse.

The responsible wife vs. the irresponsible one

Another immature type of reaction, which can be a source of serious trouble, is the wife who fails in her responsibilities. It is surprising how many calls a doctor receives from husbands asking for help in getting the wife to take her duties toward the children more seriously. The husband finds that the youngsters have been left alone in the house for hours on end while she was out shopping or with a neighbor. How many stories appear during a year about a fire where young children are burned to death while mother "stepped out only for a minute."

A more sophisticated form of this irresponsibility exists when the wife spends too much money and helps create an economic crisis, which requires her to go out and get a job. Today, with all the talk about the feminine mystique, she can marshall a great deal of support for doing this; but her real motive is to escape responsibility. This is no reflection on the real career woman, or the professional woman, who is completely aware of what she is doing and provides adequate help and ample personal attention to cover both sides of her life.

I never could tolerate the phrase, "only a housewife." I can't imagine a job or career that requires the time, effort and ability that being a wife and mother asks for. Any successful wife and mother would be capable of almost any job in the business world after having proper on-the-job training. Perhaps, because we have put mother on a pedestal, we have done her a disservice. Looking at her realistically, she is like any other career woman, some good, some bad, some settled, some not. There are mothers who bring children into my office, and

I watch them as I would study the hands of an expert surgeon.

I remember one patient years ago who brought four healthy boys, four, five, six and seven years old into my small examining room. As I stood dumbfounded, waiting for things to start flying about, she glanced around the room, picked a blank floor space along the wall, and pointing to a spot she snapped her fingers loudly. With each snap, she spoke a name in a gentle voice, "Peter, Mike, Nick, John." With each snap, a sturdy little fanny hit the floor. When the fourth was seated, mother came over and sat at the desk to have her blood pressure taken. She asked some questions, and we discussed her diet and some of her symptoms in routine fashion, and in a peaceful, leisurely manner. I kept looking out of the corner of my eye at Peter, Mike, Nick and John, expecting any minute to see a wrestling match or maybe the opposite—a group of cowed, beaten children. But no. They talked; they poked at one another a little, and in general acted as boys should; but they were always under control. When they left, their progress down the bare hall was the pure bedlam and uproar you might reasonably expect, but not the frantic release from chains sometimes seen. As they approached the reception desk, she gestured with her hand, and the noise subsided. I can still see that picture.

Although I never saw the children again, I delivered two more (both girls) for her, and I have been able to keep in touch pretty well. Judging by what her neighbors think of her, and what her boys are doing now, I think she should rank among the legion of experts. Whoever says "just a housewife" is not speaking about her. There are grades of success in all fields. Why shouldn't motherhood be the same? The best doctor runs into cases in which his ability is inadequate, and then he refers the case to someone who is more capable of handling it. Mothers should be able to recognize that they, too, may need help. Many do get help in bull sessions and coffee klatches. When true inadequacy due to immature reaction patterns is found in parental abilities, professional advice should be sought.

Infidelity

Infidelity is another immature reaction. Although I have discussed it elsewhere from other aspects, at this point I call attention to the type of infidelity which is based on a need to punish. So much of the maturing process depends on the child coming to terms with parental authority. As the person moves from parasitism to independence, the conflict between self-interest and socialization must be solved. Most of this conflict revolves around parental authority figures. The passive male and female have a tendency to use infidelity to punish authority figures. The cheating wife is trying to get even by punishing. Foolishness. Yes! That is why it is called immature or childish. Is there an excuse for misbehavior? I won't say it is or it isn't. I certainly would not argue with calling it an extenuating circumstance. This is an exception to the rule quoted earlier in which it was said that a cheating wife was not in love with her husband. The wife may really love her husband as deeply as her childish heart can love anyone. The tragedy is that when she is thrown aside and divorced, the shock and hurt forces a rapid increase in her emotional growth rate so that she learns her lesson. Again, it must be repeated: they need professional help. He needs to understand her, and she needs to understand herself.

One final word on immaturity. Most people have heard the old Latin quote, *"In vino veritas—in wine there is truth."*

Many know from first-hand experience the drunken remark that cuts to the core. Later you listen to the apology and the plea to be forgiven for hurting your feelings. What makes you uncomfortable is that the remark hit so deep and was so painfully astute that you keep wondering just how drunk the speaker really was. Alcohol releases inhibitions, and a great deal of immaturity lies just below the surface, held there by our ability to suppress the child in every man. The social drinking which is so common in our society has this rather unexpected side effect of becoming a serious source of marital conflict by opening up the Pandora's box of childhood.

7 Love

All true love is subjective and unique and at the same time creates communion. Here, as always, love of the sexes is an image of divine love which cannot be re-experienced by the outsider. It is something lonely: the lovers leave everything behind them. Yet love is not true when it is unique and lonely. It must also create community.

—*Karl Stern*, Pillar of Fire

No one can write a book on the subject of sex and not touch on the subject of love. It is particularly appropriate to follow a chapter on emotional immaturity with a discussion on something which is possible only for mature persons. The immature person cannot love any more than a newborn infant can walk. The ability to love another person does not exist until the total personality is developed. Then one has the capacity for loving neighbor, white or black, and for loving those of the past whose shoulders we stand on. To love, one must have the capacity for courage, faith and discipline.

Misconceptions about love

The hippies, the flower children, use the word "love" often, but they obviously do not understand it. Love would make them concerned about the long-term effects of drugs, and it certainly would worry them about children being born into such a haphazard home and culture. I am afraid they are falling into the trap so many are caught by. They confuse being loved with the capacity to love. Truly, as stated by Eric Fromm, love is an art that requires knowledge and effort. It is not a pleasant feeling which one "falls into" when one is lucky. Love is a verb, not a noun; it is something you do, a capacity you develop as a part of your personality, a way of feeling. Love, like most human virtues, is a rarity, hard to develop and hard to find.

My service with the infantry in Italy during World War II leaves many memories that I would just as soon forget; but I never could forget the love that existed amid the hell, and I am sure most of the men felt the same way. It sometimes seemed that we lived in an entirely different world. Part of the difficulty of readjustment was getting used to man's selfishness when the danger of imminent death was removed.

Many people think they will acquire love when they become successful, powerful or rich. Men reason this way, but women seek love by making themselves attractive. Both sexes develop rules in regard to proper conversation, being in on the "in" things, being modest, helpful, etc. The whole endeavor is a mixture of being popular and developing sex appeal. A danger inherent in this attitude is that they learn nothing about love itself. Most people believe love is simple. The real problem is to find the right object, the soulmate, the *one* for me.

It is tragic that when we broke away from the custom of choosing of marriage partners by parents or guardians, we moved into the equally irresponsible choice of love-objects. As a result of this, many of our people are faced with the same

problem presented to their Victorian ancestors. They suddenly find themselves married to a stranger, but they are not
prepared for it, and their ancestors were. How can we say
"married to a stranger"? Our young people have freedom of
choice; they pick their own partner. It was noted previously
that freedom is a big word. Our youngsters do have free
choice *if* they were free of their childhood before they made
their choice. But if the girl is marrying to escape a dominant
father, or if the boy is running away from a dominant mother,
the freedom is an illusion. He chooses an *object* to fill his
need, and when this fails, he wakes up one morning with a
stranger lying in bed next to him. This happens to all of us to
some extent, so that most married couples speak about the
honeymoon being over, or about the romantic phase dying
out; but the adult takes over from there and learns to love
the stranger with a love that grows day by day and year by
year.

Unless we make the teaching of love a part of our educational system, and unless more artists and writers rise up in
rebellion against this immense and tragic error, the consequences cannot help but become more devastating. In the
old society, with its extended family, there was much love
based on knowledge of each other and duty to the family.
In the megalopolis of the year 2000, the nuclear family will
be more isolated in the crowded mass of humanity, and the
capacity to love strangers will be even more important. If it
can generate an increased capacity for love, the monogamous family will become stronger and more capable of bearing
the expanding burdens being placed on it.

The whole idea of falling in love with an attractive object
is central to the modern so-called sexual revolution as portrayed in the playboy philosophy. The immediate gratifica-

tion of desire is particularly appealing to the immature and to the concept of love as the simple task of finding the right object. This philosophy, using the word in the sense of thinking style, fits in perfectly with the "affair." The process can be broken down into the discovery, or courtship, the illicit affair and the awakening, or "too bad you're not the one."

What happens to these people does affect us when they have children and abandon them, when they marry our daughter or son, or when, they push their ideas via the communcation media. The needs of love are forceful, and the cry is strident; but the song of love is long, and its voice is quiet. What Eric Fromm in his *Art of Loving* calls

the third error, leading to the assumption that there is nothing to be learned about love, lies in the confusion between the initial experience of 'falling in love' and the permanent state of being in love, or as we might better say, of 'standing in love.' If two people who have been strangers—as all of us are—suddenly let the wall between them break down and feel close, feel one, this moment of oneness is one of the most exhilarating, most exciting experiences in life. It is all the more wonderful and miraculous for persons who have been shut off, isolated, without love. This miracle of sudden intimacy is often facilitated if it is combined with, or initiated, sexual attraction and consummation. However, this type of love is by its very nature not lasting. The two persons become well acquainted, their intimacy loses more and more its miraculous character until their antagonism, their disappointments, their mutual boredom kill whatever is left of the initial excitement.*

What Dr. Fromm says here is absolutely true, but, for reasons previously mentioned, the value of sexual intercourse in this experience of intimacy is far more important to the man

* Eric Fromm, *The Art of Loving* (New York: Harper Bros., 1956), p. 4.

than to the woman who has not had time to reach her full sexual maturity. She may value the coital act for the intimacy it brings, not for the act itself. Or she may have acquired experience with other partners and may have developed an orgasm on a mutual masturbation level, thereby divorcing herself from the truly sexual union implied in the word "intercourse." None of the excitement of the affair should be missed in a marriage. Instead of diminishing, the growth of intimacy should go on for years, not with the rush of the honeymoon, but with the beauty of coming around the bend of a lovely river. There will be more rapids, and some will be better than the first. In a mature marriage, with a fully developed and capable person on both sides of the bed, the world can be rocked to its foundations.

Once we accept the fact that love is an art, we approach it as we would any learning project: by finding out all we can about it, and by taking every opportunity we can find to practice doing it. To learn about love, we must think about it, talk about it and do it as much as possible. What is love? To answer this question is impossible. We might as well ask ourselves, "What is life"?

According to Dr. Fromm, man's unique problem is separateness, or isolation, and he uses desparate measures to escape the anxiety engendered by an ever-increasing sense of separateness. His misuse of the sexual act, drugs and alcohol are all a part of this desperate struggle and absolute failure. To remain in this prison of aloneness means insanity. Various solutions to the problem of aloneness have been offered by different societies. Our solution used to be conformity, that is to make everyone, both men and women, equal. In recent years the younger generation seems to rely on rebellion, group living and psychic shocks of various kinds.

There is some value in avoiding aloneness by creative work where the artisan plans, produces and sees the results of his work; but this kind of productive activity is becoming scarcer with each passing year. All of these are only partial answers, and one complete answer lies in the achievement of interpersonal union-fusion with another person in love.

This desire for personal union has always been a powerful force with man, and it had to become stronger as mankind moved further away from his natural origins. This desire has always been the force behind the clan, the tribe and the family. At present it is becoming a need of critical importance. Every generation has faced disasters, most of which were massive invasions, or other cataclysms which were easy to see and difficult, yet simple, to cope with. The present crisis in separateness is more complex to understand and far more arduous to cope with. So our search for the understanding of love is more than a personal satisfaction for our people. It could mean our survival as a society. Failure to achieve interpersonal union means self-destruction or the destruction of others. We need love for existence; without love, we will have insanity.

Many of us realize that love is a matter of giving and not receiving, but we think of giving in terms of sacrifice, of giving up something. Giving is truly an act of potency. The man in the act of giving knows his strength, his wealth and his power. This experience of vitality and potency fills him with joy. Giving is more joyous than receiving, not because it is a deprivation, but because the act of giving is an expression of life. The act of sexual intercourse is a beautiful example of how our living is changed by our point of view. Understood in the above context, the male gives of his potency and his maleness with love, and he does it with the joy of living.

His wife should be able to receive his act with the same feeling; but her gift is pure love expressed in her act of reception. Her response is magnified by the joy of orgasm, compounded and abetted by love. Those women who find themselves incapable of such giving, and those who can only receive, are often called frigid; but they may only be immature.

Responsibility and love

In attempting a definition of something as complex and as difficult to understand as love, one is forced to talk about what it does and what it means. Along with implying giving, it also implies certain other elements, among which are care, responsibility and knowledge. It not only implies these factors, but it also influences them so that they can become somewhat different from what we ordinarily think of them. Loving care means an active concern for the life and growth of what we love. To care for a child is to be concerned for its food, health and comfort. We want to satisfy it and coddle it, yet we are concerned about its growth and discipline. To be concerned for a modern child means to care about preparing the child for today's world, not yesterday's. Concern recognizes the need for gentle, firm, consistent training and discipline early in life. But the same concern helps a parent to recognize when to start releasing the child to independence, when to relinquish control for guidance and, finally, when to allow the young man or woman to run free and independent.

Care and concern will lead into responsibility. To some, responsibility is a duty. In the meaning of love, responsibility is a voluntary act. It is a response to another human being, to her needs, to her problems and to her defects. One who loves is not immune to anger, frustration, jealousy and all the sins and defects of man. But when he recovers from his anger, his responsibility to her will help him to "put out his antennae," which will make him sensitive to her psychic tension and help him to sense her need.

Responsibility can be overdone. Some women try to be responsible for their husband, but because they lack respect, they become a nagging wife, a domineering person. Respect tones this down. A woman who loves her husband has concern for him as a man and respects the man she married. Her respect exerts influence on his feeling about himself, and enhances his growth as a man so that eventually she has more to respect. She loves him as he is, not as she may want him to be. As she respects him, she gets to know him better. Responsibility is not possible without knowledge; one element reinforces the other. It is really impossible to separate any of these qualities. There is too much interlocking.

Knowledge and love

For our purposes it may be helpful to look at the development of knowledge as a separate entity. In some ways knowledge is one of the key factors in the growth of love in marriage and thus in the growth of sexual responsiveness and maturity. Gaining knowledge of each other is a fascinating process, which goes on undisturbed throughout all of marriage. I can give personal testimony concerning its growth in twenty-seven years. Most of my patients have probably been married for ten to twenty years. They constantly refer with surprise to learning something new about their partners. Gaining knowledge was what I meant when I referred to sprouting antennae, or becoming sensitive. The husband who has these antennae protruding from his head picks up those wonderful little signals which tell him when to leave a party early and head for home and bed. These are the instruments you use to interpret that dirty look you received after you patted her derriere right out in public at that last dance. Antennae tell you when "No" means "No," and when "No" means "Yes." Knowledge like this helps you to know when you should call home, even though you just left, because you sense she wants to talk about something. Knowledge, concern, responsibility, respect, all filled with love, add up to living in a fully human, constantly changing and improving wonderful world, a happy marriage that results in a man and a woman becoming a couple.

Knowing is the direct path by which love allows us to escape from that frightened and anxiety-ridden state of separateness into the depth of another's being. Through that fusion with this one special person, we gain more insight and fusion into all persons. This is what so many are seeking. Although they are searching in the right place, they are not conducting the search in the proper manner. You cannot find love by wandering around looking for an object. You must search for love in yourself before you offer it to another person. The act of love is the central theme of man's search, but it must be love with respect, concern, responsibility and knowledge.

So many writers use the word love, and then they have to append the adjectives sexual love, brotherly love, motherly love, etc., to bring out what they want to discuss. In essence, all love is similar; it differs in where it is directed. A man loves his wife with a love that will be sexual at times, but most of the time it will not. A man loves his mother as he loves his wife, but this love should never be sexual in the specific sense. A man loves his brother, but this, although the same act, will be changed, because love is a dynamic, inter-acting process and brother is not mother. Love extends to all members of the human race. I may love my enemy and yet not hesitate to shoot him when I have to. I think we have trouble with that "love thine enemy" line, because we confuse liking with loving. "Certainly you have to love that man, but you don't have to like the b---," is an old joke. As an interaction, an interpersonal process, love is affected by the person toward whom it is directed. It will take on a different coloration in each situation. Not only is my love for my mother different from my love of my brother; but my love for brother Bill is somewhat different from the love I hold for brother Mike. This is due to what is called a feedback mechanism.

Assuming one has learned and accepted a theory of love similar to what has just been outlined, what can be done about it? How do people become proficient in love? Well, how do we become proficient in anything? By practice, of course. We can learn that love is a force we can direct outward. We develop the ability to discipline and train ourselves by con-centration. In all our contacts with teachers, other students, workers and friends, we try to develop and concentrate our force of loving toward them. This is an intensely personal experience and does not have to be done in any public man-ner. At first it gives us the ability to see people differently. This is not love in any foolish, sentimental sense, and it should not interfere with our ability to appraise another person real-istically. One learning to see with love will probably see more than he or she did previously. Love does not hide the evil a thief does. Love does not cover a fool's stupidity with bril-liance. Love teaches us to listen to people when they talk.

Most of us never hear one half of what others say. We are too busy thinking of what we are going to say when they finish. The concentration necessary to master this art mobilizes forces we never knew existed. It helps us develop patience to wait, watch, listen and look.

An interest in developing skill is a primary requirement for increasing the capacity to love. As this concentration of interest intensifies, the person's whole life will be changed or reorientated. His way of thinking, feeling, seeing and hearing becomes fully human, and his feeling of union with mankind deepens and broadens. Love also makes one more sensitive and aware of people, his receptors improve, and his total communication with people is better. There is greater awareness of tone of voice, facial appearance, body stance and all the other big and little things that make communication between people so much more than talking. The antennae become fully grown, and humanity opens up as the wonderful kaleidoscope it really is. This kind of living can never be dull; every moment on an elevator, a street, or in a subway becomes an adventure. People-watching becomes being with people. It is a fascinating way to live. No man who has this capacity for loving is ever alone in a crowd, and the feeling of separateness that can generate such terrible anxiety is eradicated forever.

8 Religion and sexuality

So build we up the being that we are.
—William Wordsworth

The problems discussed in this book have been viewed from the point of a doctor in relation to his patient. The fact that the doctor is a Catholic has not been a point at issue. It usually isn't in routine practice. It must be admitted that being a Catholic has some effect on how a person looks at sexuality, just as being a Frenchman or an Italian might have a greater effect. Certain problems in marriage exist for Catholics, and other problems have a different emphasis. Attention will be directed in this chapter to problems that are affected by religious beliefs.

It is foolish to think that some of the old attitudes toward sex, as seen in the history of the church, were in some way characteristic of, or unique to, the church. These attitudes were, after all, a part of Western culture, and they became more deeply entrenched in some of the Protestant churches than in the Roman Catholic Church. American Puritanism was far more anti-sexual than Roman Catholicism. There are many volumes outlining the sources of some of the early attitudes, but it is enough to admit that for hundreds of years a strong current of antisexual feeling and writing did run through much of the church's teaching on sex. St. Paul's, "Better to marry than to burn," the raising of virginity to a higher state than marriage, the definition of chaste as virgin —all are examples of this feeling. Much of this might be described as a part of preaching tradition rather than the teaching tradition; but, in terms of their influence upon people, they are ultimately of almost equal force.

The Christian life was presented as a constant struggle against the evil inclinations of the flesh—man's lower nature. Much of the early reaction against sex was based on the belief that Christ was coming back in a short time and on the terrible degradation and depravity in the surrounding world.

The church has had long experience and is painfully aware of the great and everpresent fact of sin and evil and of its consequences for the human race. She knows that sin has often led to a frightful perversion of what is in itself a noble power. It is to prevent this perversion that she calls for temperance and self-control. She is not basically opposed to the proper use of sex in marriage, but she feels that this rightful use requires self-discipline; and much of what we know of marriage and have written about it here points out the need for such self-discipline and control throughout marriage.

The Roman Church, like any institution of long duration, has accumulated a legal structure or code, and this is always slow to change, understandably so, if its role as a guide is not to be lost sight of. Some of the slowness was contributed to by the fact that the leaders were all celibate. A married clergy would have meant an earlier appreciation of some of the values of marriage, which were not recognized until recent years. The same help could have been offered by a more complete participation in religious life on the part of the lay people, as has been recommended by Vatican II.

The birth control controversy

The birth control controversy has a long and complicated history. For those interested I would recommend Dr. Noonan's *History of Contraception.**

The number of factors involved in this two-thousand-year history are too diverse and complex to discuss here. But the basis of the doctrine is vested in the classification of the purposes of human intercourse into the primary one of procreation and the secondary purpose of mutual support and love, or relief of concupiscence, as stated by older writers. This all comes together in a delineation of the natural law, which holds that the nature of a thing or an action reveals its purposes. To circumvent these purposes is to render them unnatural. Therefore, anything which interferes with the primary purpose of intercourse—procreation—renders that particular action unnatural and, therefore, illicit.

Rhythm was exempted from this rule because no illicit action was used, and the result was obtained by abstaining from any action. Any method which interferes with the passage of sperm or egg would be interdicted.

It is interesting to note that this doctrine was developed at a time when the exact nature of procreation was unknown. We have no way of knowing just what any particular group of church fathers or theologians knew of reproductive physiology at any particular time in history I have always been intrigued by an old idea called the *"homunculus* theory," which was the belief that the male semen contained thousands

* John T. Noonan, Jr., *Contraception: A History of Its Treatment by the Catholic Theologians and Canonists* (Cambridge, Mass.: Harvard University Press, 1965).

of little men which were deposited in the female to grow like seeds. It would not be hard to see how interfering with this process could be interpreted as murder.

The more liberal Catholics of the post Vatican II period have come to feel that either the natural law mechanism is inadequate for complete understanding, or that our increased knowledge regarding the nature of the human sex act requires a new understanding.

Many of the factors which are producing such rapid social changes are throwing the people of God and their institutional church into a turmoil. Changes in systems of living require new means to cope with them, and expanding knowledge requires new approaches to old doctrines and precepts. Some of the ideas about sexuality, which have been presented here, are less than one hundred, or even less than fifty years old, and are just now being put into circulation. If men and women had full awareness of female sexuality and the course of feminine sexual growth, this writing would be unwanted and useless. When and if this concept of married sexuality is completely understood and more universally agreed on, our ideas regarding birth control and the natural law will change. For many this has already occurred, despite the publication of *Humanae Vitae*.

At present, many individuals feel that the procreative and the unitary purposes of intercourse in marriage cannot be separated. They believe that there are no primary and secondary purposes, but that each purpose is part of the other. Therefore, one cannot consider an act as procreative, and therefore moral, because an essential part of its goodness and value lies in the depth of the union it fosters, and in the support it offers to the marriage and the family. Each subsequent act is also procreative, because it fosters the development of union; and this merging of the two persons into a couple is a part of the act of procreating a mature human person.

Once this is fully comprehended, it can be said that intercourse between husband and wife when the child is five years old, or any age, is just as important to that child as the original procreative act wherein the child was conceived. When this point of view is accepted, there is no basis for the interdiction of birth control. The old restrictions do not apply. In other words, our increased knowledge regarding the physiology of reproduction, and our greater awareness of the psychology and the total value of sexuality require a re-thinking of the old code. For many people, it means a greater freedom of choice in the means to regulate the number of children. Practically no one today argues against the need for responsible parenthood, but the disagreement centers on the means to be used.

Humanae Vitae

Humanae Vitae was a disappointment to many members of the Roman Catholic Church. The opening of the windows in Vatican II had led them to feel that the time had come for a new understanding of the church's people as persons, and a greater appreciation of the role of the laity in the Church— a role in which their opinion and expressions of feeling would be given serious attention. When a lay person supports his church with his full heart and soul, there must be disagreement; otherwise there is no fullness. The encyclical was a disappointment in the first place, because it was so long in coming; secondly, because it was against the advice of the majority of the Papal Commission; and lastly, because it did not answer the modern objections against the older doctrine.

It was a disappointment because so many people felt that this was the time to support humanity, not to burden it with greater strains. Depending on the conceptions of the past is not enough, because various outside structures, which were the basis of support in the past, no longer exist. The marital relationship is being asked to sustain itself from within by the persons involved. Such sustenance requires more commitment, and hence more freedom.

Certain errors, which crept into our old attitudes, persist today to confuse the issue. One of these errors was our assumption that planned parenthood was against children, or was anti-child-centered. When we Catholics speak of family limitation, we call it responsible parenthood; when we speak of the non-Catholic advocacy of the same thing, we call it birth control. Planned parenthood means the free and responsible use of the means of transmitting life, as the encyclical says, but the emphasis is on the parent's freedom from the tyranny of biology. As stated in the encyclical, "This new state of things gives rise to new questions," but the only answer given by authority is a straight "No," and the only support given is that of authority.

Part of the new state of things is our realization that for some women repeated pregnancies can mean a disintegration of the marriage, together with a growth of antipathy toward the husband and a complete destruction of sexuality as a support for the marriage. These people are told that love and faith will help them through their trials, but one of the main supports for that human love is denied them. For many of these women, their faith is expressed in a panic-ridden series of prayers and novenas to rid them of this burden. It is true that such women in the past have become saints in similar trials, but it is much more difficult today when a simple solution to their problem is at hand. The women in the past had the full support of their culture. How does a mother face this situation today when she sees her neighbors' children growing up happier, more secure in their parents' love and more upright morally than her own? What does she do when the path she has chosen under this sort of direction results in her children leaving the strife-ridden home and running headlong into promiscuity, illegitimate pregnancies or the too early marriage, which is used as a means of escape?

Certainly, as stated in the encyclical, the teaching authority has the right to interpret the moral law, but the married partners also have the responsibility to make this decision. The more astute and historically-minded lay and clerical members of the church have great respect for the long history of authority in the church, but they must also remember the gradual change of opinion on the doctrine of the use of money, and on the astronomical findings of Galileo. In both these cases the church recognized the need to adapt its doctrines to changing circumstances and knowledge.

Love in marriage is total, as the encyclical states, and it is also unique. This very totality and uniqueness prompts many to call for responsible parenthood. Couples who are growing in this totality and uniqueness do not want to use destructive measures, such as living as brother and sister. Just as a marriage which has not been consummated by sexual intercourse is not considered a true marriage, so many persons feel that a marriage where sexual intercourse must cease is no longer a marriage. As pointed out in previous chapters, one of the greatest factors in promoting a durable and faithful union, even unto death, is the very sexual intercourse, either in full or in part, which is being denied to these couples.

When the encyclical states that the unitive and procreative

meanings of the conjugal act are inseparable, most of the people who are in opposition to other sections of *Humanae Vitae* agree wholeheartedly. However, they feel that undue emphasis is placed on the biological-procreative meaning when it is said that every act must be left open to procreation. To create a situation where the unitive meaning must be abolished by the abstinence required is disruptive and contradictory. The conjugal act by its intrinsic structure unites husband and wife, but it does this whether that particular act is procreative or not. The fact that the act is intrinsically procreative in its totality is obvious in the desire of the large majority of couples for children, a desire that becomes overwhelming if indications of sterility occur. This is easily shown by the extreme efforts made by childless couples to adopt children.

The statements in the encyclical regarding conjugal infidelity, the general lowering of morality, and the loss of respect toward women are most unfortunate. They must deeply wound the millions of wonderful non-Catholic parents who have used such techniques for many years. Attempts to equate the use of contraceptives with an increase in immorality in recent years are extremely non-scientific in that they deny the existence of so many other factors.

If we desire to encourage our young to be faithful to the moral law in the world of today, we certainly had better come up with a great deal more than a simple admonition. What they must have is a greater understanding of themselves as persons and of their relation to society. They must be given a deeper understanding of sexuality so that it becomes an object of reverence and respect. This is not done in the classical attitudes expressed in the older arguments against birth control. We must show them the role of sexuality in marriage, and show them how the misuse of this gift of God harms them and their subsequent growth. We cannot expect youth to follow our arguments if we insist sex is something to treat with respect before marriage, and then degrade it afterwards by interfering with its growth and use.

One of the unfortunate occurrences in this entire controversy is that the trend toward liberalization has given many people a better look at planned parenthood in operation. For many of them, years of experience with the old restrictions are being compared with the experience of the new freedom, and the effect of the comparison has been devastating. Countless marriages have improved and, in some cases, have been salvaged, by the use of effective birth control techniques. To paraphrase Dr. John Rock, we have pulled our feet out of the mud, and we find the walking much better. The increase in love and security, and the peace and tranquility brought into the home are benefits too great and too obvious to be denied. This is why so few of my patients have changed their behavior since the promulgation of the encyclical.

The rhythm method

Rhythm, or periodic continence, is based on the fact that the female of the human species follows a menstrual cycle of roughly twenty-eight days and ovulates, usually once a month, about fourteen days before the next period. If this ideal cycle were persistent, (it rarely is), the couple could stop intercourse on the ninth day from the beginning of the period and resume on the nineteenth day. Under these conditions the plan would work fairly well, except for the fact that variations probably occur in the time of ovulation, or in the life span of the sperm or egg, so that pregnancies could occur. If a

patient had a persistent thirty-two day cycle, ovulation would
occur on the eighteenth day and intercourse would have to be
interdicted from the thirteenth to the twenty-third day. If
a patient had cycles that varied from twenty-eight to thirty-
two days, coitus would not be allowed from the ninth to the
twenty-third day.

As the cycles become more irregular, the period of abstinence becomes longer. It is obvious why rhythm can be
very difficult for some couples, and how it can be destructive
of so much that it is good and supportive in a marriage. It
seems unfair that, if this is the only system allowed in seeking
responsible parenthood, it should be so dependent on the ran-
dom variations which are present. Five days is allowed before
ovulation and five days after, because the exact length of time
in which the sperm can survive inside the body is not always
known, and neither is the survival time of the female ova
known. In addition, the days of ovulation in women are somewhat erratic, so a period of five days on each side is chosen to
provide a safety factor. If a patient varied from twenty-eight
to forty-five days, coitus would have to be avoided from the
ninth to the thirty-sixth.

Any male can recognize at a glance the difficulty of such a
system, and he will become intensely aware of it when he
attempts to live with it in marriage. He must not only learn
to control his sexual drive, but he will have much more trouble
turning it off and on. More than one wife has explained to her
doctor that her husband would rather abstain entirely than
attempt to live under this kind of restriction. The male would
also have to avoid all affectionate contact and truly live as
brother to his wife, and here the trouble starts. The woman,
particularly in the early years of her sexual development,
will have no trouble in avoiding intercourse. Her drive is

not that concrete or specific. But she cannot live without affection and relief from loneliness.

This kind of living can destroy the marriage. It may survive as a parental partnership, as a brother-sister friendship, as a dedicated life of celibacy, but not as a marriage. The meaning here can be twisted out of shape, but for those who understand the nature of a good marriage union, with its natural and full support of a developed sexuality, the statement is very clear. Few marriages can long survive a rhythm cycle where fear of pregnancy is strong and the periods are irregular.

What is to be gained from all this extreme effort and risk? The effectiveness rate is usually quoted as about seventy percent. This means that, if a thousand women use the system for one year, thirty will get pregnant. This must be compared to two pregnancies on the pills and eight pregnancies with a diaphragm.

Despite sincere and honest effort, disaster strikes in far too many cases. If the word "disaster" seems too strong, it is because the reader has not sat alone with these women, listening to their terrible crying and bitterness. The tragedy is that something as wonderful as pregnancy is allowed to become a disaster. Certainly these patients adjust to their situation and accept their children as gifts from God, but the price is very high. For some couples the system works well, and the periodic abstinence increases the value of the sexual union in their eyes. As one husband put it, "You can learn to appreciate quality instead of quantity."

If the variety of human nature and the inadequacy of pat advice or simple solutions has not become apparent in these pages, the author has failed miserably in making his thought clear. Periodic abstinence, or even more prolonged continence, has always been required of some couples, and always will be required of them. For some, it increases the depth of their regard and love for each other. For others, it creates tension and even disaster. For some couples, a total freedom to use the sexual act as frequently as they desire may produce degradation to the point where the act loses its value as a unifying force. There are many non-Catholic couples who are free to use any method they choose, and they elect to practice rhythm for various reasons. There is no doubt that, if it could be rendered more effective and more accurate, it would become highly acceptable; but the nature of the physiological changes occurring with ovulation are so gradual that this is not likely to happen.

One refinement is the use of the basal body temperature to recognize the day of ovulation. If the patient takes her temperature every morning before arising and records it on a graph, she should note a rise in temperature around the time of ovulation. This elevation of temperature occurs and remains present to the extent of about one degree until just before her period. With this method the variations in time of ovulation are indicated. One month the rise may happen on the fourteenth day of her cycle and in the next month on the nineteenth day. As a result, she may resume coitus on the nineteenth day in one month and on the twenty-fourth day in another month. Obviously, this is an improvement over resuming every month on the twenty-fourth day. It is more time-consuming and bothersome; and besides, it upsets young children who become disturbed when they see Mommy with a thermometer in her mouth, and they pester her with queries such as, "Mommy sick"?

Most couples who use this technique are assured of eight to ten days a month of rather safe time. The efficiency rate with this method is probably about eighty-five percent. The ability to utilize these two methods, or any of the techniques of artificial birth control, requires a certain amount of intelligence and motivation. Any attempts to help people in their use are time-consuming and difficult, particularly so for the people who are most in need of help—those living in the culture of poverty throughout the world. Poor people are concerned about severe and immediate problems regarding food for the day, or heat against the cold. This makes them view a problem nine or ten months off as nonexistent. Lack of training in counting or anticipation also seems to be detrimental to successful use of such techniques.

All birth control measures are difficult to establish in poverty-stricken areas, but the use of periodic abstinence or rhythm is almost impossible in such cases. These latter techniques require a tremendous motivation and a good deal of skill and attention—factors not easily found when people have to struggle so desperately for existence itself.

From the point of view of an obstetrician who has worked closely with large numbers of patients utilizing the periodic continence technique and who has followed many of these same patients into an era of a greater assumption of freedom, only one comment is possible, and that is to express amazement at the difference noted by the patients. In previous years, many patients used various artificial birth control techniques, because they had no religious beliefs which prevented their taking advantage of such methods; but they had no reason to offer any comment on this phase of their lives. As a more liberal view began to prevail, more Catholic patients discussed the problem at length, because they were unfamiliar with the methods and ill at ease with their decision. In these discussions it became apparent that there was an almost universal improvement in the marriage union, reaching into almost every aspect of the couple's life.

One of the most expressive comments I heard came from the mother of ten children who had been on the pill for six months. With a somewhat surprised look in her eyes, she said, "Doctor, do you know that for the first time in my life I feel married"?

It must be admitted that many of us who prescribed and taught the rhythm techniques did not look upon it as a medication, or as a prescription, and we neglected our responsibility to watch for side effects and dangers. Dealing with patients who are taking the progestins has changed all that, so our alertness to increased nervous tension and anxiety among patients on the pill will have to apply to patients on rhythm, too. We will be forced to require follow-up visits, to question patients as to how they are functioning as married couples, and to evaluate their program, not only in terms of effectiveness in helping them avoid pregnancy, but also as to the fulfilling of their obligations as wives and marriage partners. We will have to watch out for dangerous side effects in the disrupted and torn marriage, and the personal conflict that becomes intolerable.

We cannot assume that any husband who complains about rhythm is a sex fiend. There are marked variations in the sex drive, and what might be easy for one man can be impossible for another. One wife's need for affection and support may be so great that she keeps her husband sexually stimulated, and she cannot expect him to be continually calming down his aroused emotions. Rather than advise the ordinary couple to live as brother and sister, it would be better to recommend separation.

Today's children are much more aware of the state of emotion between father and mother, and they are upset when they find their parents sleeping in separate bedrooms. More than one couple who were attempting to do this have described the ill effect this has on even young children. They demanded to know what was wrong, or they spread it all over the neighborhood, so that friends began to make inquiries about their marital disharmony.

The need for responsible parenthood is here today and will increase in the foreseeable future. The conditions growing within our society demand it. This means that procreation must be a total commitment to the child for a period of eighteen years or more. The aim is not merely to have a baby but to produce a mature, independent, Christian adult who can truly become a child of God capable of fulfilling his or her role in our society. In order to accomplish this, we must recognize that the burden falls almost entirely on the parents, and they must form the most perfect marriage union possible for them in order to carry out this mandate. Adult human beings do not result from a simple act of biological mating. They come from a true marriage, a welding together by love of two persons into a couple. Parents who do not love each other will have difficulty in loving their children. They may be deeply concerned, but this is not enough for the child to grow on. Without love in the home, the child can become just another lost modern soul.

For many Catholics, to leave the comfortable old world of law and order is in reality to lose Camelot, a beautiful dreamworld that never existed. The rules were so well-known that all disobedience was carried on in carefully constructed compartments where it could be ignored. As a result, the most restrictive societies supported the most flourishing prostitution. Where wife and family were placed behind walls and protected most zealously, we saw *machismo* (a man is not a man until he has had a woman, and self-control means homosexuality). The father who hired guards to watch his daughter took pride in his son's escapades, and whole nations of men prided themselves on cuckolding other men, positive in their simple little minds that their own wives would remain faithful.

More materialistic cultures saw the best of its "family men" sanctioning anything in the way of entertainment as long as the contract was signed. What was supposed to be morality was in actuality simply a code of laws, and the only real problem was not getting caught. The laws were being violated so regularly that many who sincerely believed in them were imposing fear on their children to try to save them. They maintained ignorance as long as possible and called it innocence, and they implied dire happenings if the rules were violated. As a result, many of the young people grew up in fear of their own human nature and brought into adulthood a distorted personality.

There is no promise in the future that improvement will come solely because old barriers are broken. The new freedom will require great responsibility and maturity. Responsible parenthood does not mean a childish avoidance of parenthood so that parents can be free to have fun and live in perpetual childhood. Every older parent knows the heartbreak of watching the youngest child grow up, and it could be a terrible frustration if natural desires for children were put aside for foolish reasons. Regret comes when it is too late. I don't think it is possible to overemphasize that the natural desire for children is so strong that most people have had as many children as they can handle, if not more. They do this even when contraceptive techniques are readily available. There are many couples who are exceptions to this rule, but they often suffer, because they have deprived themselves of something precious.

The role of the church in our society is to be our moral guide. If she does not move into this new world, who will play her part? I know of no better expression of this than Teilhard de Chardin's in *The Divine Milieu:*

Jerusalem lift up your head! Look at the immense crowds of those who build and those who seek. All over the world men are toiling—in laboratories, in studios, in deserts, in factories, in the vast social crucible. The ferment that is taking place by their instrumentality in art and science and thought is happening for your sake. Open then your arms and your heart, like Christ your Lord, and welcome the waters, the flood and the sap of humanity. Accept it, this sap—for without its baptism you will wither, without desire, like a flower out of water; tend it, since without your sun it will disperse itself wildly in sterile shoots.*

* Pierre Teilhard de Chardin, *The Divine Milieu* (New York: Harper Bros., 1960), p. 138.

9 The masculine mystique

This is yet the childhood of the world and a supine credulity is still the most charming characteristic of man.
—Sir William Osler

There are no books on men or manhood. No one has written of the *masculine* mystique. Some comments have appeared about the "crisis" of masculinity, but little is done about it in the way of professional studies. A great deal can be said about women and man's relation to them, but what about man himself? Just how is he going to fit into today's world, or tomorrow's? What is a modern man in a personal rather than a career sense? If he is no longer to be the man of the house, just what role will he play? Who and what will the husband of the marriage of tomorrow be?

A new role for men

I believe that his role in the future will have to be an evolutionary offspring of his traditional position. He will have to do as the woman is doing—change and yet remain the same. Just as she will always be the mother, he must remain the father. His fatherhood will be suited to newer social conditions and to a changing concept of interpersonal relations. Marriage and society will always need his masculine outlook in order to remain in balance.

Perhaps all of us who have been interested in the crisis of our times will find our interest in the next few years becoming more focused on man as a husband and father. As the feminine "rebellion" which started some fifty years ago reaches a more entrenched position, the male counter-rebellion will have to occupy the spotlight. Up to the present time man has fought a delaying action with dramatic retreats and desperate defense of the old ways, but now may be the time to counterattack with new weapons.

Since one of the focal points of marriage will be the personal development of the couple, husbands are going to have to increase their knowledge and understanding of interpersonal relations. If he is to be the "take charge" person, he will have to learn to operate by communication and by insight instead of by edict. Following the old simple adage that before you can learn where you are going you must first learn where you are, man will have to become more introspective and self-analytical and learn more about himself and his present status.

Modern males are being taught and conditioned for security. Welfare state philosophy, corporate policies, preventive medicine, almost all of modern science is directed toward greater control of environment, prevention of illness or accident and general protective improvement of mankind's lot. All this is wonderful, and only a fool can question such worthwhile objectives; but only a blind man can claim that evil cannot arise from good, that man cannot create his own hell when he tries to build heaven for himself. The male is essentially a risk-taking person. Men climb mountains, sail over oceans to nowhere, launch themselves into the fantastically inhospitable and apparently useless realm of interplanetary space. Males are probers; they seek simply for the sake of seeking, because "it is there."

Love, too, is risky in that it is a leap into the unknown, and our modern boy, brought up mainly by his mother and taught from infancy not to take chances and not to hurt himself, does not feel secure in a world of insecurity. As he attempts to live this well-ordered life of security and safety, he becomes more insecure and anxiety-ridden in masculinity. He was meant to be a little stupid, foolish and stubborn. It takes a fool to climb Mount Everest and lose a hand from freezing, a fool to try experiments that everyone knows will fail, a fool to waste his life writing poetry that no one reads and painting pictures that no one cares to buy.

Society today demands results and proof of success, so how is a male to become secure in his sexuality except by exhibiting a string of victims? If society wants outward signs of success for everything, what do you do about masculine sexuality if you are not an exhibitionist? Isn't it logical that he should become insecure and anxious about this part of his personality? Almost everything in his world places him under pressure to prove himself a man and contributes to his doubts about himself. When he goes to the office, he is challenged by women, not only as actual competitors, but often as mother figures seeking to protect him and see that his life remains safe. At school he attends classes with girls of his own age who have a distinct advantage over him in that the system is run by women for passive, well-behaved women. An aggressive, masculine boy must become passive or be labelled a troublemaker. The model he will be expected to emulate, at least in school, will be the intelligent, well-behaved girl whose orientation is principally passive.

There are no models for our young men to utilize to help

them develop a self-confident sense of masculinity. A young man who did manage to find a good model would gain little support from our society when he imitated him. He may seek a hero by retreating to pioneer traditions, or cowboy movies; but he will not be able to make his hero fit into most of the niches available to him, and he will be unable to find a hero compatible with home and family. Any embryonic development of this nature will not find support in his home from mother, sister, daughter or wife. Much exposure that the masculine role receives in movies or television is not only lacking in support; it is actually destructive.

Father and husband portrayed as a bumbling idiot is hardly worth imitating. Seeing this picture before him year after year adds to the crisis in masculinity, so that his abnormal response by aggression or submission is not too surprising. The reaction may take either the form of irrationally violent behavior or undue submissiveness, and sometimes a combination of both. This may now be resulting in an increase in homosexuality.

For some men, the aggression takes the form of a compulsive pursuit of money or women as proofs of masculinity. When he has achieved his goal, he does not know what to do with either the wealth or the women he has obtained. For some, the retreat into submissiveness results in a compulsive retirement as a passive boarder and not a true participant in home life. The latter type of passivity often results in further condemnation by the wife for being a "do nothing." His mother also scolds him for not asserting himself.

A concomitant form of retreat is to withdraw into the protective mantle of the corporation with its job tenure, pension fund and action by committee or department where the only responsibility required is to play the game by the rules. The ultimate retreat, of course, is to avoid the issue of masculinity altogether and become homosexual.

Adolescent boys are often forced to preform at a pace dictated by the environment rather than at a rhythm suited to their own needs. An example of normal development speed was noted some years ago in certain minor seminaries in our area. These are high schools for the preparatory training of Catholic priests. These were day-schools where the boys lived at home with their families. Since they were preparing for a celibate life, dating was not common, although not forbidden. For about the first two and a half years of high school, the students were extremely active in sports and in various masculine group activities. Suddenly, in the spring of junior year, they discovered the wonderful world of girls and became some of the most highly skilled and dedicated girl watchers I have ever seen.

In contrast, the boys in the general school system were dating as freshmen, awkwardly and under pressure. They were not allowed to live an undisturbed masculine life and, in the opinion of at least one observer, were not quite as masculine as the boys who were allowed to proceed at their own pace. The peer group is not of much help here since they are having the same problems and are under the same pressure. Most boys cannot resist, because failure to comply means they will be branded as "queer." All the open discussion of sex today means that the young boy's sexuality is no longer a private matter; it will be discussed by friends and relatives who become concerned with what they consider any departure from the "normal" set by the local rules.

The young adult male finds that much of the blatant sex talk makes him feel exposed. Because his need of confidence is so great at this time, talking about sex at this stage is not of as much benefit to him as it may be to his more curious and mystified female counterpart.

Who is head of the house?

The male's sexual confidence is threatened particularly by two things: the changing status of women, and the growth of the other-directed society. The increased freedom of women, so that they are no longer completely dependent on men for economic security, and their open competition with men for more jobs and income has had a profound effect on the male, whose old image was based almost entirely on woman's economic inferiority and insecurity.

More than one husband today has had to face the fact that his wife earns more for the family than he does. At least, this situation occurs for a part of their life together, and it has produced some unusual results. More than one young wife of a medical student has helped him through school only to find that, when he finished his training and was able to start independent practice, he left his wife for another woman. When asked to explain this, Dr. Marion Hilliard of Montreal, answered, "Oh, that is simple. He needed another woman to make him feel tall again."

He may picture his mother as actual boss of the home, and he may be expected to treat her as such. Recently, a patient who was discussing her marriage tensions told a story about her nine-year-old, who accidentally sat in his father's chair at supper one night. When he noticed this, and was about to move, she told him Daddy wasn't coming home that night and that he could stay there and be the daddy. He answered, "I don't want to be the daddy because mommies don't like daddies."

Because of the home patterns, many boys doubt their ability to assert themselves against the mother, and so they react with aggressive hostility toward females. Naturally, a great deal of this hostility is temporarily suppressed while he is engaged in any type of sexual pursuit; but such repression is never totally successful, and relations are somewhat stormy to say the least.

Much of what is condemned as modern woman's aggressiveness is merely her forced move into the void left by the modern male's passivity. In marriage, especially, it isn't always her bossiness that is responsible for a change in their roles, as it is his lack of assertiveness and his failure to assume responsibility. Not many women object to a reasonable man being the head of the house and of the family when he assumes the responsibility as well as the glory. She will not tolerate doing the whole job herself, while she maintains the fiction that he is the head of the house. If he is the head, she loves it; but, if he isn't, she refuses to pretend that he is.

Man's search for maleness in a modern world

The growth of our other-directed society means that the male must often live up to what people expect of him. This was always true to some extent, but the modern organization man is bound to far more rules and regulations of an unofficial, but paralyzing, nature than was true some years ago. He must make almost every move of his life according to what is expected of him. Just finding out what these rules are may involve a massive amount of effort.

Many of the life factors which we have always considered to be classically masculine are missing, and the few we have left will be gone in a few more years. The spirit of adventure, the movement into the unknown, the exploring mind, are not welcome in the world of the organization man. Quests may be made and scientists may be hired, but work is done by committee. The true innovators are lonely "nuts" who never made a dime, and they are probably unknown to all but a few of the people who work with what they left us.

The other-directed society means that the male must live up to what other people expect of him, so his spirit of self-reliance atrophies. Male-to-male contact diminishes as the various male refuges disappear or are invaded by the newly-emancipated female. We render little support for any male-to-male intimacy, and we will probably give less support as the amount of homosexuality increases. Because of the increase in homosexuality, any man-to-man or boy-to-boy association becomes suspect and frowned upon. The young adolescent, with his precarious, new-found masculinity, is frightfully easy to disturb when he forms relationship with boys his own age. If such a friendship is disrupted through fear of homosexuality, he is thrown into the boy-girl arena long before he has been able to find his own masculinity.

Since much of the basis of homosexuality is fear of and antagonism against women, the results are often just the opposite of what the manipulators are seeking. The word "manipulator" is used with deliberate intent, since so many members of our freedom-conscious society are so fond of the task of overhauling other people and arranging their lives for them. The pattern of early dating and early marriage, which I hope is in the process of changing, (at least some indications seem to show this), makes sexuality a trap for the young "boy" who has not yet been able to integrate sexuality into his life. The other-directed society, with its emphasis on conformity, denies us some models which might be of benefit to our young men. We do not have enough mature bachelors to provide models for our young men. Our society looks upon any single male over thirty as sexually or psychiatrically abnormal, or we think he is tied to his mother's apron strings.

In many respects the male's role is being attacked far more severely than his sister's, and he is losing ground rapidly. Much of the rebellion in modes of dress and styles of living, which antagonize so many of the older generation, is the result of young men seeking a new masculine image. Some of them are imitating women, but many are not; so there is great variety in the "long hair" movement. At least they are going against the old current of conformity, and rebellion is a part of the masculine style. Women take up causes and can be extremely belligerent in protest, but somehow they are rarely true rebels. The Black Power movement, although imbued with a variety of elements, is a masculine rebellion; and one of its most salient characteristics is the assertion of masculinity in an often beautiful and moving way.

The role of the male in the future, as was pointed out in the beginning of this chapter, will have to be an evolutionary development stemming from his present capacities. He will remain, not so much the boss of the family, but the head of the house in the sense of a take-charge person. He will furnish the support for the structure, and he will have the good of the whole under his guidance and responsibility. He will use his masculine capabilities when and where they are needed for the good of the family, but not for personal support of a nonexistent masculinity.

In the majority of marriages, the male is often more capable of making decisions. The woman's greater awareness of the multiple facets of a situation makes it more difficult for her to reach a decision under certain conditions. Her tendency to become intensely personal about things interferes with her objectivity. It has sometimes been said that the male's stupidity is a help to him in making decisions. Because he is not aware of all the complexities, he can arrive at answers more quickly. In many cases any decisive action may be better than continued indecision and worry.

None of this is meant in a derogatory sense at all, since a woman's value in helping to bring full understanding to a problem is fully acknowledged, and the need for her way of viewing a problem is recognized. The male's ability to assert himself in a situation is exemplified in the following type of situation. Some years ago one of my patients told me that her husband had pulled her out of a rather peculiarly difficult situation. Her father was a widower living alone with the last of a succession of housekeepers. My patient was one of three daughters. Since she was the oldest, she was in charge of her father's household and housekeepers. On this particular night, in the middle of the dinner hour, she was called to the telephone where a rather long and confusing conversation with the father's housekeeper took place. It seems the housekeeper's clock had been damaged, probably by the cleaning woman; but the housekeeper was questioning the wife as though she had done it. The conversation kept becoming more and more confused, and the poor wife was actually getting hysterical trying to defend herself.

All of a sudden the husband got up from the table and walked over to the phone. Quietly taking the phone from his wife, he spoke firmly into the mouthpiece, "Please leave my wife alone." He hung up the receiver and ushered his wife back to the table where he politely helped her into her chair.

I am sure any group of wives can come up with countless

similar stories where male decision has been of life-saving
value in the midst of female indecision. The male who learns
to use this ability with intelligence and discretion will find
that his family depends on him. He will fill his role as head
of the family in a natural manner and will not have to resort
to so many false gestures of support for his ego as men of
previous generations did.

Another factor in his makeup that can be of use to him is
his ability and inclination to plan ahead. He may be somewhat
blind to what should be obvious dangers right under his nose,
but he is usually well aware of what a college education is
going to cost. The smart man learns to rely on his wife for
decisions and support in areas where her competence is better
than his and to assert himself when his talents are more formid-
able. None of the classical male talents of logic, long-range
vision, or stick-to-itiveness, are distributed to all men, any
more than intuitive good sense about people, or patience in
dealing with children is given to all women. In those cases
where the wife happens to have certain gifts that her husband
does not have, it should be no problem if he accedes to her
superiority from a secure position of masculinity. In fact, the
question of head of the house and masculine assertion does
not have any relation to superiority or inferiority. The concept of antagonism is as irrelevent here as trying to decide
whether the heart or the brain is more important to the human
body. This is not a problem of rivalry to be solved by a contest; it is a case of complementary persons fitting into a new
organism, a couple. The mutuality of the roles is far more
complicated than the relation between the brain and the
heart whose functions are set by their structure. Roles are
never stereotyped, and the male exerts his masculinity by his
maleness, with all its variety and changes, not by following

any pattern established by others. He uses the qualities that lie within himself.

The male role as the support in a marriage can be played in countless ways as infinite in their variety as is man himself. He is often seen at his best in situations where disaster has struck at the marriage, such as the death of a newborn baby or a young child. For me, masculinity stands out strongest in the support I have seen so many husbands give a grief-stricken wife. I do not mean the silly, sentimental everything-will-be-all-right approach, but the firm arm around the shoulder, the careful questioning he puts me through to find out why and what so he can answer her, the visit he pays to the office later with her to talk things over. All this represents manhood at its finest. I see it as often in the 120-pound office clerk as I do in the 210-pound fullback.

The male's role as the support of a marriage is not linked to the competition of being number one in any manner. It is related to his role as the director, or the energizer, of the marriage. He is the one who will have to keep track of the state of things, to remain aware of where it is heading. He will be the one to watch for trouble and attempt to devise ways of handling it before it gets out of hand.

In his present state of insecurity, his defense mechanisms are so strong that it is almost impossible to get him to face facts without suing him for divorce and separate maintenance. For obvious reasons, I do not recommend separation for any couples unless the situation is beyond repair. Oddly enough, in some cases I have found that this is the only way to make some men admit to trouble. In one case a husband practically refused to discuss the situation with his very desperate wife until he was nailed with a rather heavy support payment in a separate maintenance suit. He suddenly woke up to the fact that marriage really is for keeps: and he was forced to admit that all marriages are indissoluble, and that remarriage is only a form of vertical polygamy where you are allowed a second or third wife consecutively, not concurrently. Since he could not afford two wives, he was forced to go back to the first.

The union had been badly disrupted by the events leading up to the separation, so when his wife asked my advice about taking him back, I suggested that she date him and follow the policy of wait-and-see. If he was able to win her over again and make her want him back for himself, as well as for the children, it might work out. He carried it off beautifully, and now, six years after the separation, they are still doing well.

If the male is to become a driving force in marriage, if he expects to be in a position to review its state and condition, to lay plans for its future growth and development, to be able to initiate discussion of its problems and to probe for trouble before breakdowns occur, he will have to acquire an inner strength of masculinity, of confidence in himself as a man, and of security in his self-image. He must not depend on remnants from the past to sustain him. After all, isn't much of the spectator sport mania merely an imitation of the day when men earned their living by physical ability and power?

I am sure that of the fantastically large numbers of guns bought each year in this country, a large number are never fired. Although man can purchase the trappings of masculinity so easily, he should not be misled into thinking they will give him any support. Among the outer trappings that can be purchased are the playboy bunnies and all the similar items. Again, this is a false and even desperate maneuver that is doomed to failure and further diminution of his image.

Another of the trappings he attempts to aquire is skill in marriage technique. His quest for marriage manuals which explain just how to do it, and in great detail, is just another of the devices which, even when memorized in detail, produce little or no benefits. His search for maleness must be directed to the realm of the spirit, and his accomplishments will lie in the deepest centers of interpersonal relationships. He will find himself in his growth as a human person and in the full maturity of his own being in relation to others both male and female.

The concept of complementariness does not mean that a man requires sexual relations to fulfill himself as a man. It means that true masculinity is found in man's relations to other men and women, not as sexual figures but as total persons. A woman can extend the range of a man's experience, but she cannot make him into a man. She may help him understand himself and his world a little better, but she cannot supply what is not there in the first place. Marriage should never be asked to render therapeutic service, but men and women do grow bigger as individuals in their life as a couple. Part of this growth in marriage comes in the pain and suffering that is a part of all marriages but which is ignored in the promotional literature. Quoting Eugene C. Kennedy, M.M.:

Only the (person) who has plumbed the depths of relating to a flesh and blood kinsman in the human condition, and learned to give without possessing, and to enter the world of the other, willing to pay the personal cost of reverencing the other's personality; only he has learned that real love is full of pain, that genuine maturity is hard-bought, and that this is at the core of understanding life itself. . . . Real love is full of living and dying; it is a long-term investment that takes the best that a person is, because it takes all that a person is.*

* Eugene C. Kennedy, M.M., *Fashion Me a People: Man, Woman, and the Church* (New York: Sheed & Ward, Inc., 1967), pp. 62, 63.

Man must live with his masculinity. He is physiologically constructed to be the sexual aggressor, so the core of his sexuality will hinge on his remaining an activist, a take charge person. He is a doer, a builder who loves to live with his creations and to contemplate the results of his efforts. He is ridden with curiosity and forces himself to accumulate all kinds of useless information. He is a thinker and a planner who builds his life on dreams and who will often give his life in an effort to make them come true. He lifts his eyes to far horizons and high mountains and stumbles over the crack in the sidewalk under his feet. He can stand as tall as the towering pines one moment and feel as small as the tiniest child in the next.

He needs to stand alone, but he must have the hand of a woman to guide him in those terrible moments which come to every life. He will try to use a woman to build up his masculinity, but he will despise her if she lets him. He needs sons and daughters, but he may never learn to realize this until it is too late. His creative and developmental capacities enable him to bring out much that is good in a woman, but often he is afraid to use these abilities.

As a father he is a model for his sons, but he is a maker of little girls into women, if he can only learn to realize his own strength. Strength is one thing he must have. In a world which no longer wants or needs physical power, he must use his strength in other ways. Fortitude or courage is still badly needed to live, either in the affluent society or the welfare state, because we remain mortal creatures, heirs to many ills; and the one who can remain standing in the middle of disaster will always be the head of the family.

Because of his balanced hormone physiology and other supporting physical factors, the male has many natural supports in this quest. If he can realign his goals, drop off some of his fraudulent supports, and apply his fortitude to rebuilding his life to fit modern conditions and modern marriage, both he and his wife will grow as persons, and then their bed will flourish.

10 Marriage and the future

Your eyes shall be opened, and ye shall be as gods, knowing good and evil.

—*Genesis 2:5*

Whatever we do at this crossroads in the evolution of man must be done with an eye to the future. Although no one can see what is in store for us, we can predict with a fair amount of reliability some of the directions that our society may take. We can see some of the choices that lie ahead and make plans for various contingencies. The future development of marriage and its tightly-knit, nuclear family has two possible directions. Marriage will continue to exist and may become even more important; or it will pass out of existence and some entirely new structure will takes its place. If the second alternative, some new structure appears, it will be necessary to completely rebuild our society, our political structure and our cities. There are no signs of this appearing anywhere in the world except under unusual local conditions.

It will be interesting to see whether the Israeli kibbutz survives after the pressure of daily invasion is removed. A major scientific breakthrough in the field of reproductive physiology would cause upheaval, but this is only in sight on a small scale with experimental animals. If it ever becomes possible, it will be centuries in the future. The reference here is to development and growth of the human fetus outside the maternal environment, or "bottle babies," if you will.

The dissolution of marriage as an institution does not appear to be a likely possibility Although the matter deserves observation and consideration, it does not require any planning at this stage of social evolution.

The first alternative, that of the survival and increasing necessity of marriage is by far the most likely path.

The family is the key to social stability

The future development and growth of marriage is a question of major importance everywhere. This is so, because the family remains the major factor in fostering the growth and development of new individuals, and almost every problem arising from personal behavior can be traced back to the family. President John F. Kennedy would be alive today if it were not for a family problem. The crisis in our cities would not be of such serious proportions if it were not for problems among the poor families in our ghettos. I am not implying that the family is the cause of all troubles, or that the parents are the root of all evil, but that the family becomes the focal point where trouble can fester for years only to boil up and overwhelm others.

Economic structures develop and educational systems grow so that the Negro male receives an inadequate education and can never obtain steady, prideful employment. Add this situation to his already degraded status inherited from slavery, and we have the development of what Ozzie Davis has called the "Negro castration complex," and he cannot function as head of the house. All of this culminates in a massive destruction of Negro family life, and a vicious circle is set up which will require massive efforts to break. Ordinary educational methods cannot possibly cope with large numbers of children from such disturbed environments, so that school systems and police are asked to attempt more and more to provide something which usually comes from parents dedicated to each other and to their children.

There is no indication that the years ahead will see anything except the continuing isolation of families and the development of more nuclear and less extended family units. This is true, because the few remaining extended units are either rural or ethnic, and both of these backgrounds are disappearing. Farm families are disappearing because the economic status of the family farm is changing, and is becoming less tenable as years go by and farms are broken by death and taxes. Closely knit families with strong ethnic ties are disappearing, because time itself destroys them as memories of the old country fade away in the minds of succeeding generations.

The move toward isolation within the family structure is accompanied by increasing isolation in the work area. The depersonalization of large corporations and governmental bureaucracy is a fact of life here and now, and there are no indications of any basic changes. Many attempts are made to combat this, but all are piecemeal efforts rather artificially contrived and of rather short duration.

City structure and home-building practices all combine to increase this isolation, usually because the customers want it this way. People living in crowded cities seek to escape the crowds and the streets with their dangerous cars and criminals of various kinds, so they move to that nest in the suburbs where the wife has no one to talk to but children, and the husband leaves at seven in the morning and comes home at seven in the evening. All the old, friendly candy stores, taverns and delicatessens are gone. They have been replaced by shopping plazas where you can be lonely in the crowd.

As the isolation and loneliness increase, where will a person seek communion with another? As separatedness becomes more prevalent everywhere else, would it not be expected that people would look for deeper and more satisfactory unions in marriage? Much of the sex play, alcholism, drug use and desperate search for pleasure, which are interpreted as signs of a decaying society, are misdirected attempts to solve these problems. As their failure becomes more apparent, marriage is being asked to fill this role.

If this assessment of the future is correct, we will expect marriage to do nothing, or to do a great deal more than it has done in the past. The family must become the most stable part of our social structure. It must assert itself as the refuge of any real depth relationships and become the core and center of our education in terms of providing the education of our young as human beings. Schools will exist to furnish the technical training, to supplement the humanizing of the young and to assist parents in the diagnosis and handling of special problems. Marriage and parenthood must and will become as respected as other professions. In the future I hope that no woman will ever describe herself as "only a housewife."

Psychiatric casebooks and juvenile court records show many case histories of people who were competent in professional fields or in business activities and yet were failures as parents. In some cases they made errors that seem so obvious as to be almost ridiculous if the consequences were not so tragic.

One of the first requirements for professional competence

is that the person take his role seriously. If a license were needed to have children, or an examination had to be passed before marriage were permitted, how would most of us fare? One of the dilemmas faced by many court authorities today is the realization that a troubled child is living in an impossible home environment. In the first place, courts are not really equipped to remove such children from these environments, because the legal machinery is not readily available. In the second place, foster homes or institutional care cannot guarantee any improvement.

The only solution which holds any hope is a combination of education and propaganda. Education in high school and college should be geared toward marriage and perenthood, not only as separate courses, but as a part of present courses in sociology, psychology or wherever a marriage course is applicable. Propaganda in the sense of public support through the various media should also be used. This is already done to a great extent and will merely have to become more organized and efficient.

No general improvement in marriage as an educational institution or as a place where deep personal involvement is possible will be conceivable without a general betterment in all of our social institutions and in our people themselves. The change required in personal development is mainly one of greater emotional depth and maturity, and much of what is happening today is fostering immaturity rather than the opposite. I hope that the destructiveness of this trend will become apparent and thereby impose self-limitation on these tendencies.

One of the greatest factors in helping to make us aware of just what is happening is truth—hard and complete. Some efforts are being made in this direction, and I hope more will be made.

A recent movie called "Phoebe," is a simple story of a girl who has recently discovered she is pregnant. The author describes her day with the boy who is an unknowing father, a day in which she is determined to tell him, but finds she cannot. After saying goodbye to him, she calls him on the telephone to tell him. The approach is soft, subtle and completely valid, and the film makes a good impression on girls.

I doubt if this movie would have much effect on boys of high school age. They would have to be hit harder and with sharper weapons to penetrate their tougher hides. Boys need to be educated more fully as to responsibility for parenthood, because they have such a long history of irresponsibility.

In contrast to this honest approach is the type of film about a couple who are punished when they sneak out at a local dance and become trapped in a fire.

We should be more interested in the self-destruction inherent in the action itself, not in the bolt from on high, because the destruction inherent in the action is far more terrible than the disasterous happenings of some of the older tales.

No artist would ever be capable of portraying the sum total of the pain, self-torture and unhappiness resulting from the venereal disease epidemic among the flower children of San Francisco. How long would you have to wait and watch the children of these children born in Haight-Ashbury to write their story?

As our society continues its process of rapid change, we will have to develop more swift and certain procedures of adaptation. None of us likes the idea of control, particularly when applied to something as personal and unique as love.

But as the family becomes more burdened with responsibility, both from within and from without, what happens in one family affects all society to some extent. It certainly did in the case of Lee Oswald's family.

In past years sex education was designed to help persons; in the future it will also be needed to help society. How can we reach consensus on such a controversial and delicate problem? Today's methods are merely stopgap measures thrown in desperately to plug up gaps in our knowledge. In what way do we go about teaching young people that sex is not the same as sexuality? How can we bring immature souls to consider that this overwhelming urge is merely a part of growing up, and it must be controlled and allowed to grow as part of a balanced peresonality lest the whole be distorted. To allow it to go unchecked is as bad as allowing pride to overwhelm you, or shame, or fear, or any other aspect of personality. Sex is merely physiological or biological; it is what happens to the body as a result of sexual activity.

Sexuality, however, is something vastly different. This is a whole portion of our personality that arises because of our reproductive system. It is a part of maleness or femaleness. This maleness or femaleness is imprinted within us from the moment of our conception and never loses its influence. It exists in us at birth. Because of it, we learn more about our sex every moment of our lives from infancy on. It colors all our relations with others, and theirs with us. We learn it from touch, from the feel of body contact, from the tone of voice. A boy learns about it from the way his father holds him as compared to the feel of his mother's arms. Beyond this he learns to know the feeling of love as compared to concern.

Man is just beginning to extend his knowledge into this area, and it will take time to learn all the methods necessary for studying behavior to this depth; but beginnings are being made with animals and children, and more will come. As we learn to define sexuality properly, we will not be so ashamed of helping our children learn about it; and we will be able to educate them in a balanced way of growing. In the past we were fearful, and we either avoided the subject or became overly technical. There were parents who advocated teaching the total reproductive physiology to a five-year-old. They thought that, because the child knew all the right labels, he or she was well informed. This was often another method of getting rid of responsibility; they gave sex instruction to the child in one large, overwhelming dose and then forgot about it, secure in the self-delusion that they had done their job. The failure of this technique is becoming more apparent, and parents are beginning to realize that like all learning, sex education is something you help your child to live with. Sex is there; I am a boy, or I am a girl, and this is good. We are parents; we kiss and we hold each other, and this is good. This is where it belongs—in marriage.

As children grow older, the value placed on the sexual relationship makes it easier for them to understand the reasons for restricting their behavior. The problems they meet in trying to do so can be discussed with their parents, who are not frightened of vague concepts of sin, or the shame of unwed motherhood. But they are frightened of the damage the boy or girl can do to themselves or to others. There is no positive assurance that children who have learned about sex in this way will do better than others did in the past; but they certainly can do no worse, and it is possible they have already largely succeeded—to what extent we are not likely to find out for some time yet.

One final note: during the time I was writing the last chapter of this book, a patient who was complaining of her difficulty in marriage mentioned having read a number of books like mine. She said that the author discussed marital relations up to a certain point, and then dropped the subject. I wondered if I had quit too soon also; but then I realized that no one can blueprint another person's life for them, let alone two lives. A book is a place to get ideas, to make comparisons with others, and to learn a little; but sexuality in marriage is living; and living is only done by being alive, by being human. No one can put life in a book. The bigger, more human a person you become, the more your bed will flourish.

As a conclusion, it might be well to attempt some analysis of future possibilities as far as marriage and other sexual relationships are concerned. Any attempt to view the future is obviously hazardous. However, forecasts based on trends that are already apparent may have some validity. In any event, they can help us understand our present position and avoid undue anxiety when and if the forecasts come true. Stating that something may come about should not be considered as approval or disapproval.

The practice of medicine gives one a unique perspective. A good physician accepts reality. Early in his career he learns that his feelings about the evil of a particular illness have no influence on the outcome for the patient. A cure for cancer will be found not by the scientist dedicated to the cause of ridding humanity of this terrible scourge, but by some stubborn workers who are faced with a fascinating problem. Men who cannot rest until they find the answer to their puzzle will discover the cure. Then the writers will descend upon them and talk about their service to humanity. However, the men who worked steadily at the problem know, and we know, that humanity is served best by those who seek knowledge and truth. Victory belongs to all those nameless ones who failed as well as to those who succeeded; and they know that their success rests on countless little victories and defeats that were noted by only a few at the time.

Population growth

Most observers agree that some long-term growth in population is bound to occur, although there may be argument as to just how explosive it will be. The recent drop in the birth rate may slow the growth rate down, but it will not greatly influence it over a long term, unless the trend remains. The population charts show that, despite ups and downs, the general trend in this country has been upward, with only occasional variations as to time and place.

Inherent in the prospect of increasing population is the Chardinian concept of hominization, or the alternative of self-annihilation, which happens with certain animal species. Hominization, to paraphrase Chardin's beautiful and complex explanation, means that the more people there are in an area, the more human they must become if they want to survive.

Much of what has been said before has involved the future of marriage, but it might be well to summarize a little before discussing alternatives. Most of the discussion has been from an evolutionary, rather than a revolutionary, viewpoint. I have said that marriage in the future is likely to become more nuclear, as well as more essential to society. Increased mobility of our population will add to the physical separation of grandparents, uncles and aunts. The family unit of husband, wife and children will become increasingly isolated, and hence increasingly responsible for filling the unique cultural and educational role, which no other structure seems capable of doing. The one note which must be injected here is that man will have to face his responsibility for creating his own society, since the tools for doing so are being developed. Once a tool is invented, no one can ever prevent its being used.

Space does not allow a complete presentation of this subject, but it is obvious that improved treatment of diabetes, which is an inheritable disease, will result in longer lives for diabetics and the birth of more diabetics. Increasing the life span will result in more problems in caring for the aged. Extensive use of efficient birth control techniques may mean that the more capable and intelligent portions of the population will slow down their own replacement rate, while the least capable increase their share of the population. If such factors are inheritable, even in part, the long-term effects might be destructive to society.

If the compression effect of increased population density is going to create tension and strain, some change in structure seems inevitable, and it is questionable whether there will be time to allow the usual processes of evolutionary development to function. Failures on the part of small groups in the past resulting in the death and annihilation of a tribe, city or nation were of little consequence to mankind as a whole because of the isolation of units. Progress was so slow and varied that survival-oriented traditions of other groups could become accepted and incorporated as part of mankind's heritage. The increased rate of change characteristic of the past fifty years, and the more rapid rate expected in the next fifty, means that things are moving too fast for adequate testing by the older methods.

Our greater communications means that we are fast becoming more alike, because no group is isolated for long. So we are more likely to stand or fall together. This would probably be true even though we had not developed such a fantastically efficient capability of destroying ourselves.

In many ways, one world is inevitable sociologically and culturally, even if not politically. All this means that the need for social planning may arise, and we may no longer be able to, or want to, let nature take its course. If this is true, careful observation of changes will be necessary, and a great amount of study will be required to determine the direction of the changes occurring and our need or ability to shape these directions. This is a task that is so complex and difficult that it would be easy to assume its impossibility if it were not for some of the things the younger generation is doing in laboratories and other crucibles of progress at this moment.

In this context, the Catholic Church, if it is to fulfill its mission, must remain relevant to society as a whole and must not allow itself to become separate and ghetto-minded. To do this we must think, speak and act in an existentialist contact with those around us of other faiths and beliefs. The world cannot be molded to the image we want. God is the complexity of complexities, and he who thinks he can speak for God in the natural order knows little of the natural order and less of God. The crisis which so many believers are going through today is in a large part due to the simple fact that they thought they had God's world all figured out. Now that they are faced with the unfolding reality of God's creation itself in the explosion of knowledge revealed in the last two hundred years, they cannot face its awesomeness and complexity. This is a part of Chardin's noosphere, and it is not a very comfortable place; but the saints have always told us that getting to know God was a terrible experience.

Loneliness

Megalopolis will place a greater emphasis on privacy than our present cities do, and the need for personal unions in marriage will become greater. Our modern suburbanities are complaining about the lack of privacy in some housing areas, while others complain of their isolation. This paradox is not too difficult to resolve if you stop to think that we all like to have certain people drop in. We all tolerate a certain number of persons for a limited span of time, but we do not like invasions, particularly by large numbers who stay too long. One suburban housewife is lonesome in her kitchen at eleven in the morning, just dying to have that nice woman two doors down drop in, while another is seething because this coffee klatch has been going since nine-thirty, and those two characters from across the street have found the liquor and are starting a cocktail party before she can get her work done.

Incidentally, it is conceivable that certain customs could evolve, or be created, which would mitigate such contretemps. They have existed in the past and probably still function in some places. It could be that man may have to find modern equivalents and test them to see that they continue to function.

The loneliness of urban life is peculiar in that the city dwellers do not so much desire privacy as much as they resent the massive and indiscriminate invasion, which occurs when the doors are left open. Some of these women are literally starving for company, but they want some control over who it will be, when it will happen, and for how long.

One of my patients once told me how much she missed the delicatessen in her old neighborhood where she could drop in and buy some small item, and in exchange receive a few words of adult conversation to balance the din of childish babble. Many of the men are sitting in their chairs reading the paper, and they are eager for the right person to talk to, not that noisy crowd who drink too much and stay so late that a guy can't keep his eyes open at work the next day.

As a consequence of this increasing loneliness, marriage is asked to provide deep interpersonal relationships to fill the vacuum left by the absence of other significant people. This may not be an improvement; it may actually be the opposite. Many of the strains and breakdowns in marriage seen in our offices, clinics and courts are due to the inherent weaknesses in this particular union, which is overwhelmed by being asked to do too much. The number of breakdowns will increase unless something is done to provide better preparation and selection, and to improve social mechanisms for reasonable contact between people. In other words, substitutes will have to be found for the aunts and uncles of the past; some method will be required to offer surrogate parents for the disruptions inherent in child-parent relations, and to provide help for the parents whose capabilities are somewhat less than is needed. If by some chance we can develop a style of urban living which would provide greater personal relatedness with an increased number of significant people, a great deal of tension and anxiety might be alleviated; but at present there seem to be very few, if any, such movements or mechanisms in sight. Many groups exist among the young adult generation, such as the "underground church" and study clubs; but they have never been able to expand, and they are limited to a specific type of intellectually curious person who will always find some involvement with people.

Neighborhood taverns serve as clubs and meeting places, but various factors, both economic and social, are making them less effective. Most churches, of whatever denomination, have a rural background and are not fulfilling this role in modern urban society despite heroic efforts on the part of some to make them fit. We seem to lack the proper tools for the job, and we need to take a long, hard look at our equipment.

Another, perhaps not so obvious, trend is that marriage will assume far more, and not less, significance in rearing children. Many of the factors mentioned in previous paragraphs apply here. As the numbers of adults available for the child to relate to diminishes, the significance of the parents becomes greater. No evidence has been developed to show that schools or other agencies can have any appreciable influence on the phychological, moral or cultural portions of a child's personality. Even in structures such as the Israeli kibbutz, researchers found that it was absolutely vital that the parents play with the baby and the child in the evenings, and that the child see the parents working nearby during the day. Since these were small and separated communities driven inward upon themselves by intense outside pressures, conclusions drawn from their experience are not necessarily valid elsewhere.

Perhaps the increasing problems of certain teen-age elements, and particularly those who are most dependent on themselves and their separatist peer groups or subcultures, are a part of the isolation mechanism. Because significant adults are not present, and because there are large numbers of ineffective marriages, more and more youngsters are being compelled to seek their own world. Perhaps we are reading the first chapters of the real *Lord of the Flies*.

This view of the evolution of marriage into a more intensely personal union fits in closely with our increasing realization that men need love, and a great deal of it. A world which has found the capability of destroying itself in a fraction of an instant must find the ability to help two people learn to love and understand each other. If this cannot be done, we certainly cannot expect the peoples of the earth to love and understand each other. Without love and understanding, we are lost, because force and fear have outlived their usefulness. A disease cannot be eradicated or prevented without first curing the patient, and armies cannot be abolished until you eliminate policemen. So peace on earth isn't possible until we have peace in our homes.

If marriage is to become more important, it must receive greater support by more extensive and more adequate preparation. This means, of course, that sex education will have to become an integral part of the whole school program from kindergarten through college. Unless a firm base is established very early, it is almost impossible to make marriage education truly meaningful. This is why this book has been written from the viewpoint of a doctor rather than a Catholic. I firmly believe that my being a Catholic makes a difference, but I certainly hope this will add to the book's value for a non-Catholic reader, rather than detract from it.

In marriage courses we should be talking about making marriage work, about why it can fail, about how a couple can build toward a more soul-satisfying union, and not about negative aspects such as rules, regulations and divorce. It is interesting to note that church rules never really forbade divorce, they forbade only remarriage. The Catholic Church said a person is allowed only one attempt at marriage unless death supervenes. Looked at in this manner, the rule makes more sense and is easier to defend than the proposition that a union which is totally destructive to both adults, and to all the children, must be maintained at all costs.

I have sometimes felt that certain marriages can only be

saved by a good, honest divorce lawyer. An emotionally immature husband who abuses his wife and children with his
total irresponsibility can grow up rather suddenly when he
finds that his flippant statement about getting another wife is
countered with a court order for alimony and support amount-
ing to three-fourths of his pay check. When he is faced with
the realization that you are not really allowed to get rid of
your first wife, but you are granted the right to support two
wives if you can afford it, he grows up in a hurry.

Educational support for marriage should come from the
mass communications media and from the arts. Much of this
is already being done, and, even though some of us resent in-
truders who seem "hung up" on sex, the general trend is improving. As scholarship improves in various related fields, the
media will have more significant things to say. The medical
profession cannot be too critical of others, since it was only
about the time that work on this book was started that the
first journal on human sexuality was published for physicians.

Social engineering

Another possible support in the future might come from a field
which really does not exist at present, although it is being
used as a part of many other scholastic disciplines and in
politics. This is what I would term social engineering. Before
the reader rises in wrath, it would be well to point out that
this means people-oriented, not state-oriented, social engineering. We already have a great deal of this around in certain
forms, such as the income tax, inheritance taxes, urban renewal
and the poverty programs, to name only a few; but much of
this has been applied haphazardly and with little or no con-

sideration for long-term results, or what doctors would call side effects.

Studying man is a relatively new science and one that is terribly burdened with fears and fantasies. It is hoped that in our lifetime we will see such studies begin to emerge as a respectable method of handling the problem. The development of computers for collecting, storing and collating information is already making these studies possible. In the past it was not possible to find out how men really felt about something, or whether they agreed or disagreed with a particular action. As a result, authority and direction were often resented as arbitrary or tyrannical. Today, techniques are becoming available for sampling and collecting information so as to give accurate knowledge regarding the popular support or rejection of certain problems or solutions.

A new balance should be developed in the various behavioral sciences to restore the importance of research material of an observation nature, so that this can be melded with the more "scientific" statistical studies so popular at present. It would help also if more people could become sophisticated enough to understand that Kinsey's data refers to approximately five thousand American men who answered questions and not to the "American male."

More revolutionary changes would have to involve the breakdown of the marriage structure as we now know it. This would seem to be beyond our capacity to predict, since there is at present little or no evidence of the directions which might be taken. A society such as ours could not survive after breakdown of the marriage contract, and something entirely new would have to take its place. Discussion of such possibilities seems to lie in the realm of science fiction.

Another possibility is the splintering of sexual unions into different forms. At present our culture (middle class American) accepts only the married and the single state. Other unions such as the common-law wife of the culture of poverty, the mistress in certain elements of European society and the more open acceptance of prostitution in some other countries already exist, but they are not officially accepted.

Scandinavia may be more tolerant of premarital experience but does not actually recognize such temporary liaisons socially. The possibility that such various unions could become more acceptable does exist. If this does happen, marriage may become more difficult to contract, and it may become more protected and respected because of its child-rearing function. Just how these unions would serve humanity or the individual is hard to say, and great care should be taken to determine the extent and severity of any side effects which could develop.

Communal type organizations have so far been insignificant, because there are only a few of them, and they exist for a particular reason, and in response to a specific situation; so that their relatedness and value to society at large seems questionable. I would inject an entirely personal opinion at this point by stating that anything involving sexual unions between a variety of partners has the danger of increasing the exposure to venereal disease and can pose a difficult public health problem, despite our present success with the antibiotics. The biological basis of these drugs is primarily suppressive, and the organism's tendency to adapt genetically provides immunity against the drug's power after a certain length of time. This might eventually result in a race between the inventiveness of the chemists and the organism's adaptability, a race the chemists are almost certain to lose.

Almost every conceivable change in our basic marriage

structure seems to be unacceptable, because the side effects, the long-term results and the failures are much too dangerous for society to tolerate. The drug proposed for the cure would do more harm than the disease it is supposed to eradicate, and, obviously, this would be unacceptable.

The future of marriage is seen as one of growth, an expansion whose outline seems apparent, but whose specific branches or postures are, like all growing things, subject to distortion or death. Man's future contains what Chardin calls "the incredible potential of unexpectedness accumulated in the spirit of the earth,"* and we must learn to live with it and use it. To do this, and to survive, we have to use what has caused the trouble in the first place—man's mind. Only by being more and more human in every conceivable sense can we keep pace. We are part of a stream whose beginnings reach back one and a half million years, and whose future drifts onward perhaps a trillion years more. The only direction we can see is that we move toward a human era wherein man becomes more important to man. He is the cause of our troubles and the solution. We have been afraid to look him in the face and have buried ourselves in other matters.

"We find man at the bottom, man at the top, and, still more, man at the center . . . man who lives and struggles desperately in us and around us. We shall have to come to grips with him sooner or later."† When we do, we will find that all we really have to do is to know him and to love him.

* Pierre Teilhard de Chardin, *The Phenomenon of Man* (New York: Harper and Bros., 1959), p. 281.
† *Ibid.*

Date Due

MY 21 '70				
AG 1 '70				
RESERVE MR CONNOR 9/1-70				
MR 21 '70				